THE PERSIAN GULF AND IRAQI WARS

CHRONICLE OF AMERICA'S WARS

Lawrence J. Zwier and Matthew S. Weltig

LERNER PUBLICATIONS COMPANY

MINNEAPOLIS

CHAPTER PHOTO CAPTIONS

Introduction: Iraqis drag Saddam Hussein's statue through the streets of Baghdad on April 18, 2003, after U.S.-led coalition troops take over the city.

Chapter 1: The Euphrates River flows through Iraq and empties into the Persian (Arabian) Gulf.

Chapter 2: An Iraqi tank crosses the Shatt al-Arab into Iran during the Iran-Iraq War of 1980.

Chapter 3: Kuwait City, Kuwait, shown here before the invasion, put up little resistance in the Iraqi takeover on August 2, 1990.

Chapter 4: U.S. president George H. W. Bush meets with Saudi foreign minister Prince Saud al-Faisal on August 16, 1990, to discuss stationing U.S. troops in Saudi Arabia.

Chapter 5: Coalition forces bomb Baghdad at night on January 17, 1991, launching Operation Desert Storm.

Chapter 6: U.S. soldiers prepare to fight a ground war in Iraq on January 26, 1991.

Chapter 7: An Iraqi woman and two small children walk through the rubble of a building in Karbala, Iraq, destroyed by Iraqi troops during the Shiite rebellion of 1991.

Chapter 8: Military and rescue workers stand amid the wreckage of the September 11, 2001, terrorist attacks on New York City.

Chapter 9: On May 1, 2003, President George W. Bush declared mission accomplished in Iraq from aboard the USS *Abraham Lincoln,* cruising off the coast of California.

Epilogue: U.S. ambassador Paul Bremer shakes hands with new Iraqi interim (temporary) president Sheikh Ghazi Ajil al-Yawar during a ceremony to transfer power to Iraq's interim government on June 28, 2004.

Lerner Publications Company
A division of Lerner Publishing Group
241 First Avenue North
Minneapolis, MN 55401

Website address: www.lernerbooks.com

Library of Congress Cataloging-in-Publication Data

Zwier, Lawrence J.
    The Persian Gulf and Iraqi wars / by Lawrence J. Zwier and Matthew Scott Weltig.
      p.   cm. — (Chronicle of America's wars)
    Includes bibliographical references and index.
    Contents: The cradle of civilization — A deadly standoff — The invasion of Kuwait — Desert Shield — Desert Storm begins — The ground war — The war goes cold — Going after Saddam — Occupying Iraq.
    ISBN: 0–8225–0848–6 (lib. bdg. : alk. paper)
    1. Persian Gulf War, 1991—Juvenile literature. 2. Iraq War, 2003—Juvenile literature. [1. Persian Gulf War, 1991. 2. Iraq War, 2003.] I. Weltig, Matthew Scott. II. Title. III. Series.
  DS79.72.Z89 2005
  956.7044′2—dc22   2003026080

Manufactured in the United States of America
1 2 3 4 5 6 – JR – 10 09 08 07 06 05

TABLE OF CONTENTS

INTRODUCTION

Baghdad, Iraq, was hot, dusty, noisy, and dangerous on April 9, 2003. Foreigners in tanks—Americans—rolled through the wide streets. President Saddam Hussein's image stared down from billboards and bank buildings and police stations.

Iraqis tried to stay out of view. Some may have felt threatened by Saddam's looming portraits. For decades, his secret police, the Mukhabarat, had kept close watch on ordinary citizens. The slightest criticism of Saddam could mean arrest, torture, and death. Most Iraqis stayed inside to avoid being hit by stray bullets. Sometimes, a crackle of rifle fire would erupt and ping against the armor plating of an M1-A1 Abrams tank. Bullets slammed

into tea shops, mosques, and parked cars. The tanks rolled right on, undisturbed, as if passing through a cloud of gnats.

Baghdad had been without electricity or telephone service for several days. The only people who could call outside the city were the journalists in the Palestine Hotel and rich Iraqis with satellite phones. The only way to watch TV (broadcast from Kuwait or Damascus, Syria) was to find someone with a diesel-powered generator and enough fuel to run it. But the news swept through the city: The Americans are here. Saddam is gone. It was hard for anyone to believe that Saddam, the ultimate survivor, could be gone.

In Firdos (Paradise) Square in downtown Baghdad, a crowd of Iraqis gathered

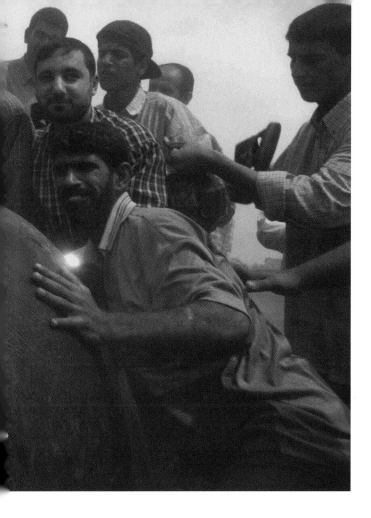

beside a convoy of U.S. tanks and armored personnel carriers. They looked around. No Iraqi soldiers. Someone started chanting, "Down with Saddam." More voices joined the chant. Words that could not have been whispered a day earlier were being shouted out in Firdos Square.

No one planned anything, but the crowd somehow knew what they would do. The 40-foot statue of Saddam with his right arm outstretched would have to come down. A few people pushed on the hollow statue. Others leaned a ladder against it, climbed up, and tied ropes around it. Someone else swung a sledgehammer at Saddam's feet.

Then a U.S. Marine, wearing sand-colored desert gear, shimmied up the statue. At first, the crowd thought it was funny, but then they saw what he planned to do. He draped an American flag over Saddam's head. The chanting crowd fell silent. Removing Saddam was fine, but the U.S. flag was another matter. The marine soon realized his mistake. He fumbled with the flag, removed it, and scurried down to ground level again.

Soon the crowd returned to the business of toppling the statue, helped along by marines, who wrapped a chain around Saddam and pulled him from his pedestal. The rest of the party belonged to the Iraqis. While some dragged Saddam's likeness through the dusty streets, others hit it with the soles of their shoes in a traditional Arab gesture of disrespect.

U.S. soldiers were in Baghdad. Iraqis were free to shoe-whack Saddam Hussein. Decades of war and hardship had led Iraqis to this moment. Hundreds of thousands of their relatives had died in Saddam's wars against Iran, Kuwait, and a U.S.-led alliance. The U.S. soldiers had brought an end to Saddam's dictatorship, but would they really bring a better life for Iraqis as they promised?

THE CRADLE
1 OF CIVILIZATION

A narrow body of water separates the Arabian Peninsula from the mainland of southwest Asia. This arm of the sea is sometimes called the Persian Gulf, but it is called the Arabian Gulf in Arab nations. To avoid offense, outsiders familiar with the region usually call it simply the Gulf.

The waters of the Gulf fill a low area in the eastern part of a large basin, a land formation shaped something like a bowl. The far edges of the basin are mountain ranges in Turkey to the north, Syria, Lebanon, and western Saudi Arabia to the west, Yemen and Oman to the south, and Iran to the east. This region is commonly called the Middle East.

OIL AND WATER

This basin contains some very valuable resources—oil and freshwater. The eight nations with Gulf shorelines (Iraq, Iran, Oman, the United Arab Emirates, Qatar, Bahrain, Saudi Arabia, and Kuwait) together have more than half of the world's known, easily removed oil under their territory.

Even though southwest Asia is generally a dry region, the highlands of Turkey and Iran receive moderate amounts of rain and snow. Two especially important rivers, the Tigris and the Euphrates, originate in Turkey and flow south through present-day Iraq. In southern Iraq, they join to form a single waterway, called the Shatt al-Arab. The Shatt al-Arab empties into the northern end of the Gulf near a point where the borders of Iraq, Iran, and Kuwait come together. Iran and Kuwait share no land border, only an offshore border in the waters of the Gulf.

In ancient times, the land between the Tigris and the Euphrates came to be called Mesopotamia. In Mesopotamia the rivers provided not only freshwater but also fertile soil from spring floods. Farther east in Iran (also called Persia), mountain valleys receive water from smaller local streams. These water resources helped great civilizations grow in Mesopotamia and Persia.

BABYLON AND PERSIA

Iraq is sometimes called the Cradle of Civilization because Mesopotamia nourished some of the earliest-known farming settlements. One of the world's most useful grains, wheat, was probably first grown there. By about 3200 B.C., a great civilization, Sumer, centered on cities in south-central Iraq.

The Sumerian civilization eventually came under attack from people living farther north and west who built a city called Babylon. These first Babylonian conquerors were Semitic peoples, from the same culture-language family as Arabs and Hebrews. From about 1790 to 1750 B.C., King Hammurabi ruled Babylon under a code of law that is still admired. Later, the hanging gardens of Babylon, built in the seventh century B.C., were so famously beautiful that they were considered one of the Seven Wonders of the World.

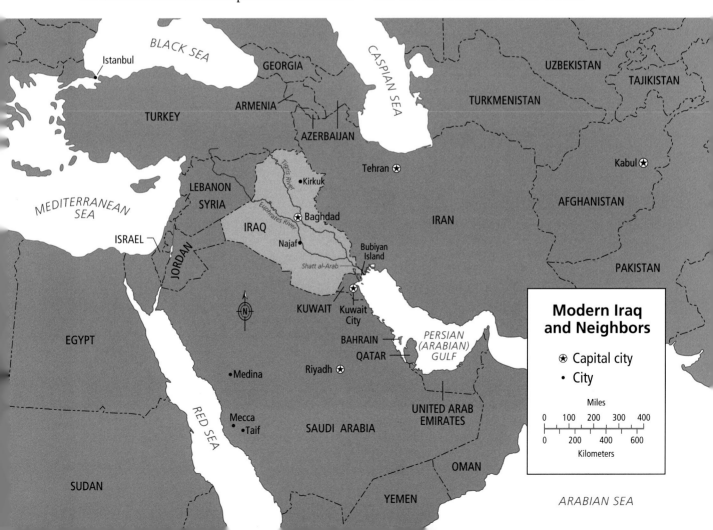

Sumerian Achievements

Although much of Mesopotamia's land was barren desert, the civilization that developed there was a fertile ground for invention. Sumer gave birth to a wide range of technologies that we use even 5,000 years later. In addition to what was possibly the first writing system in the world (see clay tablet at right), Sumerian achievements included:

- clay bricks
- the potter's wheel
- boat sails
- schools
- an extensive system of irrigation
- a well-developed code of law

In the sixth century B.C., another great empire, that of the Persians, arose in present-day Iran. The Persians were an Indo-European people. The Persian Empire, under Cyrus the Great, conquered Babylon in 538 B.C. In 330 B.C., Alexander the Great's forces marched east from Macedonia (in northern Greece) and invaded most of the lands controlled by Persia.

Mesopotamia and neighboring lands then came under the rule of various empires based to the west—including the Greeks and the Romans. A turning point in the struggle for control of these lands came with the establishment and growth of a new religion, Islam.

THE ISLAMIC EMPIRE

In A.D. 622, Muhammad, a 51-year-old trader from Mecca in western Arabia, fled from his hometown and took refuge in the city of Medina. He and his followers were escaping enemies who wanted to destroy

his newly organized religious group, the Muslims. Muhammad claimed that an angel had revealed the will of God (Allah) to him. Tradition says that Muhammad dictated these revelations to scribes (professional writers) whose transcriptions were collected in a book known as the Holy Quran (Koran—the Islamic book of holy writings). The Quran and the example

The Prophets

Muslims revere Muhammad not as a god but as the greatest prophet, a human who received messages from Allah. He is considered the last in a series of prophets that also includes such figures as Abraham, Moses, and Jesus from the Jewish and Christian bibles. Muhammad's journey from Mecca to Medina is called the hegira, and the year in which it occurred marks the first year of the Islamic calendar.

of Muhammad's life became the basis of this new religion.

Believers in this new faith spread out from Medina. Islamic armies conquered most of the Arabian Peninsula and adjoining lands, which then converted to Islam. The armies took Babylon in 641 and overran most of Persia by about 650. Over the next 100 years, Arabs established Islam as the main religion in a huge swath of territory from Spain in the west to Afghanistan in the east. Many of the newly converted Muslims in these lands were not Arab, but Arab dress, customs, and language were tightly connected to Islam and spread with the religion. This was even the case among the Persians, traditional rivals of Semitic peoples and their cultures.

A SPLIT IN ISLAM

Muhammad died in 632. Disagreements over who would be the caliph, or successor, began almost immediately. When the third caliph, Uthman, died in 656, a prominent leader named Ali claimed the post. He was both a cousin and a son-in-law to the Prophet Muhammad. The people who supported Ali called themselves the Shia ul-Ali (the Party of Ali). Ali's claim was challenged by another leader named Muawiya. In 661 Ali was murdered and Muawiya became caliph. This widened the division between Ali's followers, the Shia, or Shiites, and the followers of Muawiya, who were called the Sunni.

In 750 the capital of Islam moved to Baghdad, in present-day Iraq. A new age of achievement for Arabic culture began. Under the patronage (support) of the Baghdad caliphs, some of the world's best

A Mongol manuscript from the late 1400s depicts the life of Ali. Followers of Ali are Shiite Muslims.

mathematicians, medical doctors, chemists, astronomers, philosophers, and other scholars preserved ancient learning and made important new discoveries.

This era ended in 1258, when Mongol invaders from the northeast, led by Hulagu Khan, captured Baghdad, slaughtered most of the residents, and destroyed the city's grand buildings and canals. For almost 400 years afterward, Iraq was conquered and reconquered by various armies. The next longstanding rulers were the Ottomans, a Turkish-speaking group based in what became Istanbul, who captured Baghdad in 1638. With only brief interruptions, Ottoman rule over Iraq continued until 1917. During this time, Baghdad was the capital of a province within the Ottoman Empire, and the territory of Kuwait was officially controlled by Iraq. The members of the Kuwaiti royal family were allowed to remain in their palaces as long as they obeyed orders issued by the empire.

During World War I (1914–1918), the Ottoman Empire joined Germany in fighting Britain, France, and their allies, including the United States. After the war ended with the defeat of Germany, the Ottoman Empire broke apart. A new international organization called the League of Nations gave Britain a mandate (governing control) over Iraq, Kuwait, and other parts of the region. To settle border disputes among Iraq, Kuwait, and Saudi Arabia, a British team under Sir Percy Cox drew up new borders.

Cox's borders turned out to be very important. For one thing, they gave Iraq only a very small coastline on the Gulf (about 38 miles), much of which is blocked

Sir Percy Cox

from the open Gulf waters by Kuwait's Bubiyan Island. For another, the Cox plan set the southernmost border between Iran and Iraq at midstream in the Shatt al-Arab. The two historic rivals, Arab Iraq and Persian Iran, would have to share this vital outlet to the sea. Finally, the lines Cox drew in the desert determined which countries had oil and how much they had.

OIL PRODUCTION STARTS

The first successful oil well in the Gulf region was drilled in southwestern Iran in 1908. The invention of the automobile with an engine that runs on gasoline made oil a valuable resource. The first discovery of oil in Iraq was in 1927, near the north-

An early Iraqi oil operation on the Shatt al-Arab in the 1920s. The discovery of oil in the Gulf region sparked great interest from oil companies in Europe and the United States.

Colonel Abdul Salam Arif *(waving, right)* addresses a group of supporters in Najaf, Iraq, explaining his plans for reform after the overthrow of King Faisal II on June 14, 1958.

ern city of Kirkuk. Kuwait's first well began producing oil in 1938. Oil companies from Britain, France, Germany, the Netherlands, and the United States struck deals with ruling families throughout the Gulf region for permission to pump and sell oil.

In 1932 the British granted Iraq full independence under the government of King Faisal I. He died the following year and was succeeded by his son, Ghazi. King Ghazi believed Kuwait should be part of Iraq, and in 1939 his troops moved to the border. They were apparently ready to invade, but King Ghazi died in a car accident, and the invasion never occurred. World War II (1939–1945) followed soon afterward. The generally pro-British monarchy of Iraq managed to hold onto power.

On July 14, 1958, a group of army officers staged a coup (overthrow) of the government of Ghazi's son, King Faisal II. Abdul Karim Qassem and Abdul Salam Arif were leaders of the rebellion, and Qassem became the new prime minister. Immediately, he was the target of a number of assassination attempts. The second assassination attempt in 1959 was organized by a political group called the Baath Party. The Baath assassination squad included a young man named Saddam Hussein. The attempt failed. Some of the plotters were captured and served time in prison, but Saddam fled to Syria, then to Egypt.

On June 19, 1961, Kuwait became fully independent from Great Britain. The Kuwaiti government was led by the al-Sabah family, who had been Kuwaiti rulers since 1752. The leader of Kuwait is an emir (prince) chosen by the royal family from among its younger members after the death of the previous emir. At the time of independence, the emir was Sheikh Abdullah al-Salim al-Sabah.

Iraq immediately restated its claim that Kuwait was Iraqi territory. Threatening once again to invade Kuwait in late June

Saddam Hussein *(right)* became vice president of Iraq in 1968.

1961, Iraq was forced to withdraw when Britain sent troops back to Kuwait. The Arab League, a group of Arab nations that Iraq had helped establish in 1945, accepted Kuwait as a new member. Since other Arab nations were dealing with Kuwait as an independent nation, Iraq was under pressure to do the same. In October 1963, Iraq's government signed an agreement that recognized Kuwait's independence. However, Iraq continued to claim that its border with Kuwait had never been established by international agreements.

In 1963 Abdul Karim Qassem's opponents finally succeeded in assassinating him. Power struggles led to several shifts in Iraq's leadership in the following years. When Saddam Hussein's cousin, Ahmed Hassan al-Bakr, became president in 1968,

Arabic Names

Writers using a shortened form of Saddam Hussein's name usually refer to him as "Saddam," not "Hussein." This is correct, because Saddam's name follows one of the most common patterns among Arabic names: the second part of his name, Hussein, is the name of his father, not a family name.

In some parts of the Arabic-speaking world, particularly the Arabian Peninsula, it is common to put *bin* or *ibn* ("son of") or *binti* ("daughter of") before the father's name. Other Arab people include a clan name, a professional name, or a place name usually beginning with "al-" in their names.

Saddam was already a leader in the Baath Party, and he became vice president.

As vice president, Saddam was in charge of the police and the military. He used his position to increase his power and to pave the way for his control of the government and of the people. Opponents of the new government were publicly hanged. Dissidents, those who disagreed with Baath Party policy, were purged—they were removed from office or they were killed or imprisoned by the security forces that Saddam controlled. Saddam did not want these security forces to have a chance to turn against him. So he purged them as well and set up a new set of security forces. One branch of these new forces was the dreaded Mukhabarat. This secret police watched over the other security forces as well as over the public. In addition to removing from power those who opposed him, Saddam surrounded himself with people he knew and trusted. Most of these were Sunni

Saddam's Early Life

Saddam Hussein was born in northern Iraq on April 28, 1937, to a poor Sunni family in a small village outside of a poor town, Tikrit. His father, Hussein al-Majid, died before Saddam was born. For the first several years of his life, Saddam was raised by his mother and her new husband. Saddam's stepfather was violent and abusive. When his stepfather and mother could no longer afford to take care of him, he went to live with his uncle, Khairalla Talfa.

Young Saddam was deeply influenced by his uncle, who held strongly racist opinions. He despised Jews, Iranians, and Westerners. In the 1950s, the family moved to Baghdad. It was there, as a teenager, that Saddam became involved in politics.

Muslims from his home region near Tikrit. With the party fully under his control, Saddam was able to work on removing Ahmed al-Bakr's support within the government and set himself up as successor.

In July 1979, al-Bakr stepped aside, making Saddam president. Saddam maintained power through tight control of the police and his Mukhabarat and through the ruthless destruction of any opposition. He ordered thousands of Shiites and members of other opposition groups killed. He spent government money to develop Tikrit, an area that had been poor during his childhood.

Also in 1979, a revolution occurred in Iran. Students, intellectuals, and religious parties had united in a popular uprising. The conservative religious leaders felt that the shah's (king's) attempts to modernize the country violated Islamic law. The shah, Mohammed Reza Pahlevi, was overthrown and fled Iran. An ayatollah (religious official) named Ruhollah Khomeini returned to Iran after 15 years of exile in Iraq and France to lead the country. Iran became an Islamic state ruled by Shiite Muslim religious leaders. The former shah of Iran went to the United States in October to receive treatment for cancer.

A majority of Iranians wanted the shah returned to Iran to face trial for alleged cruelty during his reign. They had been suspicious of the United States for urging the shah to pursue Western-style modernization. They were furious that the United States seemed ready to welcome their former ruler. The already strong anti-American feeling in Iran grew even stronger. On November 4, 1979, a crowd of about 500 Iranian civilians, shouting "Death to America," stormed the U.S. Embassy in Iran's capital city, Tehran. They subdued the marine guards, took control of the compound, and captured 66 U.S. citizens inside.

As 1980 dawned, the Gulf region was in turmoil. Iran and Iraq had strong governments eager to expand their influence. But the two nations distrusted each other. Saddam Hussein's government worried that the Iranian revolution would inspire a revolt by Iraq's own Shiites. The Shiites outnumbered the Sunnis in Iraq but had little power in the government. Ayatollah Khomeini's government in Iran, inspired by the success of its Islamic revolution, wanted to spread the revolution to other countries. The Gulf region's two most populous countries were on a collision course.

A DEADLY STANDOFF

On September 22, 1980, Iraqi fighter-bombers struck air bases throughout Iran. Small platoons of Iraqi raiders captured Iranian territory along northern and central sections of the border. The main attack came in the south. Using portable bridges, Iraq transported armored fighting vehicles and thousands of soldiers across the Shatt al-Arab. They seized the oil-rich province of Khuzestan in southwestern Iran and occupied the eastern bank of the Shatt al-Arab. This gave Iraq control over both sides of the long-disputed waterway.

Saddam had hoped to catch Iran at a weak moment and score a quick victory. Iran's armed forces were still recovering from the loss of their most experienced officers, many of whom had been purged during the revolution for having ties to the shah. The hostage crisis at the U.S. Embassy in Tehran still preoccupied Iran's leaders. As long as Iran and the United States were bitter enemies, Iran could get few spare parts for the U.S.-made weapons the shah's government had bought.

Despite these attacks, Iran was not defeated. The Iranians settled their hostage crisis with the United States by releasing the remaining captives on January 20, 1981. Ayatollah Khomeini's government went on to release many jailed fighter pilots, whose return made the military stronger. Iran also began using "human wave" attacks. In these

Blindfolded U.S. Embassy hostages were photographed on the first day of their capture in November 1979. Iran finally released all of the hostages more than a year later. The hostage crisis soured relations between Iran and the United States.

attacks, tens of thousands of new recruits, some as young as nine years old and many of them unarmed, stormed positions held by Iraqi invaders. By mid-1982, Iran had won back almost all the land captured by Iraq and went on to gain control of territory in southern and eastern Iraq.

Shifting Advantages

At the beginning of the Iran-Iraq War, Iran seemed to have the advantage. Iran had more fighters who were dedicated to and inspired by their Islamic revolution. Yet Iraq was able to raise more money for buying weapons and paying for the other costs of war. Neighboring countries such as Saudi Arabia, Jordan, and Kuwait, which are populated mostly by Sunni Muslims, willingly lent money to Sunni-controlled Iraq. They feared that if Iran won the war, the Shiite majority in Iraq would welcome a strict Islamic government in that country.

FOR ONE SIDE OR BOTH

Among its supporters, Iran counted some Arab nations, such as Syria and Yemen, which had disagreements with Iraq. Most Arab nations, however, worried about religious uprisings in their countries and hoped for an Iraqi victory. They provided Iraq with money and weapons. During the war, Kuwait lent Iraq the equivalent of U.S. $20 billion. Saudi Arabia contributed almost as much.

At the start of the war, the United States had poor relations with both countries. The United States considered Iraq an ally of the Soviet Union (a Russian-led superpower,

1917–1991), which was the leading rival of the United States for power and influence around the globe. And the 1979 revolution and hostage crisis in Iran had created a deep division between Iran and the United States.

Gradually, the United States leaned toward favoring Iraq. The U.S. government feared a spread of the Iranian religious revolution more than it disliked Iraq. If Iraq could keep Iran in check, Americans might benefit. In 1984 the United States urged countries around the world to stop shipping arms to Iran. Later that year, the governments of the United States and Iraq reestablished relations.

EYEWITNESS QUOTE: POISON GAS ATTACKS

"I could see a cloud with a dark yellowish color spread into the village. I could see from far away the animals were dying, but I could not see anybody at that time standing up or walking around at the time the blast happened. But I could smell something like garlic and my mouth tasted bitter and it became difficult to breathe. After the cloud disappeared, we went down and saw that a lot of animals—birds, goats, sheep, cats, mules — were dead. And we saw a lot of people dead."

—a Kurdish survivor of the 1988 gas attacks

CHEMICAL WEAPONS

At several points in the war, Iraq was accused of using chemical weapons against Iran. Chemical weapons are usually a kind of gas, liquid, or powder that can be sprayed over a wide area to make people sick or kill them. Some of the accusations against Iraq were later supported by international investigators. For example, it was clear that Iraq had used chemical weapons in March 1984 against Hoor-ul-Huzwaizeh, an Iranian village. The best-known chemical attack during the war, however, was by the Iraqi government against some of its own citizens, the Kurds of northern Iraq, in 1988.

Kurdish children and their families fled Iraq following the chemical weapon attacks on their village by the Iraqi government in 1988. They found shelter at a refugee camp in Turkey.

The United Nations

On October 24, 1945—at the end of World War II—representatives from 50 nations signed an agreement creating the organization called the United Nations (UN). Its charter declared that these nations were resolved to work toward peace, respect for universal human rights, observance of international law, and social progress.

The United Nations has its headquarters in New York City. It represents 191 member countries and works toward many goals. These goals include fighting the spread of disease, protecting the environment, opposing terrorism, protecting the weak, aiding the special needs of Africa, and preserving the goals of the original 1945 charter.

The United Nations includes two councils. In the General Assembly, every member country has a vote. A simple majority is all that is necessary to pass a measure. In the other, the Security Council, membership is limited to 15 nations at any one time. Russia, China, France, Great Britain, and the United States are permanent members of the Security Council. The other nine seats rotate, a year at a time, among the other UN member states. For a resolution to pass the Security Council, it must receive at least nine votes and not be vetoed (voted against) by any of the five permanent members.

The Kurds live in the mountains straddling the borders of Iran, Iraq, and Turkey. They have their own language, Kurdish, and their own customs. Many of them hope to establish an independent nation of Kurdistan. Some had organized into groups of *peshmurga* ("those who confront death") to fight for their freedom. Saddam Hussein saw Iraq's Kurds as a powerful threat to his rule. Saddam's forces struck hard on March 16, 1988, by spraying poison gas over Iraqi Kurds in the town of Halabja. About 5,000 Kurds died in the attack.

NO WINNERS

The Iran-Iraq War ended on August 20, 1988, after both nations accepted a UN resolution (statement) calling for an end to hostilities. The war had claimed at least 300,000 Iraqi lives and at least 500,000 on the Iranian side. Because oil wells became prime targets for destruction, the war cut deeply into each country's earnings from oil exports. Eight years of war changed no borders and removed no governments. It was a very expensive and deadly eight-year stalemate.

3 THE INVASION OF KUWAIT

After their war, Iran and Iraq struggled to rebuild their crippled oil industries. Iraq had borrowed tens of billions of dollars from its neighbors to fight Iran and could not pay its debts. Postwar Iraq had another problem: a leftover army of more than 500,000 soldiers, who suddenly had no war to fight and no jobs to go back to.

Saddam Hussein tried to shift the blame for Iraq's troubles onto other countries, even some that had aided Iraq during the war. He repeatedly complained that Kuwait was selling too much oil to the world market, which kept the price of oil low. This low oil price was very harmful to Iraq, which had almost no other source of wealth. Saddam said he would use military force against

Kuwait unless the Kuwaitis cut their oil production. To back up such threats, he moved about 30,000 troops to the Kuwaiti border.

This crisis seemed to pass after Kuwait agreed within a week to cut oil production and started discussions about payments to Iraq for lost oil revenue. The president of Egypt, Hosni Mubarak, mediated between the two nations. Mubarak said that Saddam had personally promised him not to invade Kuwait. These personal assurances were passed on to George H. W. Bush, who had been elected president of the United States in 1988.

On July 25, 1990, Saddam Hussein summoned April Glaspie, the U.S. ambassador in Baghdad, to his office. He accused

The Glaspie Meeting

The written transcript from April Glaspie's 1990 meeting with Saddam Hussein seemed to indicate U.S. acceptance of Iraq's warlike stance. However, Glaspie herself later claimed that the transcript had been doctored by the Iraqis. She said that she had stated that the United States would defend its friends in the Gulf and that she had warned the Iraqis that all settlements must be made peacefully.

the United States of plotting against Iraq and described the United States as a weak country that would not go to war because it would be unable to face the death of its soldiers. Ambassador Glaspie replied by restating that the United States hoped for closer relations with Iraq. She also said the United States did not want to take sides in any border disputes among Arab nations. These latter remarks were later criticized in the United States and elsewhere. They seemed to imply that the United States would stand aside if Iraq invaded Kuwait. Glaspie disputed this interpretation.

Satellite photos taken by the U.S. Central Intelligence Agency (CIA) from late July and August 1, 1990, showed a vast increase in Iraq's forces along the Kuwait border. Yet President Bush and other world leaders showed little concern. Iraq had made such shows of force along the border before. Bush believed they meant only to scare Kuwait.

THE ONE-DAY TAKEOVER

At about one o'clock in the morning on August 2, 1990, hundreds of Iraqi tanks and about 100,000 Iraqi troops crossed the desert into Kuwait. They were only the first wave of an invasion force that was soon to number at least 200,000. In a single day, Iraq's advance force easily seized its small but very rich southern neighbor.

The first Iraqi troops reached the capital, Kuwait City, within a few hours. They met almost no organized resistance along the way. Kuwait had only a small army (about 16,000 troops), a small navy, and a modest air force. They were not prepared for a full-scale invasion by Iraq's army, which was probably the fourth largest in the world.

Some Kuwaiti fighter pilots raced their French-made Mirage jets into the air, but almost none of them tried to battle Iraq's fighters. Instead, they flew to Saudi Arabia to preserve at least part of Kuwait's air force. Any military hardware left behind in Kuwait was destroyed or seized by the Iraqis. Kuwaiti soldiers who remained in uniform quickly became prisoners of war or were executed by Iraqi raiders. Large numbers of Kuwaiti soldiers and police officers ditched their uniforms, hid their weapons, and tried to blend in with the general population.

Kuwait's emir, Sheikh Jaber al-Ahmed al-Sabah, fled to Saudi Arabia, eventually taking up residence in Taif, Saudi Arabia's summer capital. Most of the emir's government also fled the country or went into hiding. When Iraqi forces attacked the emir's Dasman Palace in Kuwait City, only one high-level government official remained. The head of Kuwait's Olympic Committee, Sheikh Fahd al-Sabah (a brother of the emir), raked the Iraqi troops with automatic-rifle fire from the palace steps before being gunned down.

Calls for help were going out from Kuwaiti leaders fleeing for their lives and from Kuwaiti diplomats in foreign countries. They pressed other Arab leaders and the world community for support against Iraq. The most urgent pleas were addressed to the United States. The crown prince, next in line to become Kuwait's emir, called the U.S. Embassy in Kuwait City for help at around daybreak—twice. The embassy, he was told, was a small installation with only a few marine guards. They could do nothing against the advancing Iraqis. Kuwait's ambassador to the United States also called for military support from the United States.

President Bush went to sleep that evening knowing that Kuwait had been overrun by Iraq. He was unsure what to do about it. Iraq's motives and future plans were unknown. He wondered whether the United States should risk its soldiers and its national prestige in an attempt to rescue Kuwait. Bush also weighed the very practical question of whether the United States could drive Iraq out of Kuwait.

A PROBLEM OF DISTANCE

On August 4, President Bush sounded firm as he declared, "This will not stand, this invasion of Kuwait." In reality, at that time

> ### EYEWITNESS QUOTE: A 13-YEAR-OLD IN KUWAIT
>
> "[When I heard about the invasion,] I picked up a copy of the Holy Quran that was about as thick as my arm and began to pace the apartment with it mumbling a prayer I don't remember anymore. . . . I can't remember much else from that day, apart from the pacing and the running around of Mom and Dad and the phone calls they made. The lines were cut two or three days later."
>
> —Kemal Bosnak, Turkish-Jordanian resident of Kuwait, 1990

the United States had no way to pressure Iraq to leave Kuwait.

An effective operation against Iraq would require hundreds of thousands of soldiers and a staggering amount of military hardware. The United States would also need a base of operations near or on the Iraqi border. No large U.S. military bases were in the area. The closest long-term U.S. base was on the island of Diego Garcia in the Indian Ocean, about 3,000 miles away.

Saudi Arabia is the only country other than Iraq to have a land border with Kuwait. It was the obvious choice for a U.S. base. But President Bush was told early in the crisis that U.S. troops were not welcome. Without access to Saudi territory, a decisive U.S. attack against Iraq was nearly impossible.

Saudi Arabia's King Fahd was generally pro-American, but he feared an outcry from other Islamic countries if he publicly allowed U.S. troops into the kingdom. Two of Islam's holiest sites, Mecca (the Prophet Muhammad's hometown) and Medina (his city of refuge), are in the western Saudi province of Hejaz. Many Muslims would be insulted if U.S. troops set up camp in Saudi Arabia, the holy land of Islam. The U.S. troops would be mostly non-Muslims, who would eat, wash, and speak in ways contrary to the rules of the Quran. The troops

The Conflict between Israel and Palestine

Palestine refers to the area that roughly includes modern Israel and part of Jordan. Palestinians are the Arabs who live in or whose families come from Palestine. The area of Palestine has been important to the Christian, Islamic, and Jewish religions since they began. Many places there are considered holy by all three religions.

Christians, Muslims, and Jews have lived in Palestine for centuries. Yet in modern times, Palestine has become one of the world's hot spots for ethnic and religious conflict. In the early 1900s, the number of Jewish people who moved to Palestine began to increase. Called Zionists, they were seeking a new Jewish homeland in the land the Jews had settled in Old Testament times. After World War I, the League of Nations gave Great Britain control of Palestine. Under the British, even more Zionists settled there. Many native Palestinians opposed this Jewish immigration, and differences about how to share the sites holy to both Judaism and Islam led to protests and violence.

Even more Jewish immigrants began to settle in Palestine after World War II. Many were European Jews who fled from the areas where their friends and relatives had suffered and died under Nazi Germany's rule. The United States encouraged Great Britain to accept this idea. As problems between the Palestinians and the Jews mounted, Britain turned the situation over to the United Nations. At first, the United Nations tried to divide Palestine into two parts, a Jewish part and a Palestinian part. However, neither side agreed with the division. In 1948 the Jewish group declared its settlements the Nation of Israel. Soon after, Israel was attacked by armies of the Arab Palestinians, as well as neighboring nations in the Arab League, including Iraq, Jordan, Egypt, and Syria. Israel quickly defeated them and controlled most of Palestine.

The Arab League told the Palestinians that they should leave Israel and await the full Arab conquest of Israel, after which Palestinians could return home. Many listened and left. A new Palestinian organization, the Palestine Liberation Organization (the PLO) was created to work toward returning the land of Israel to the Palestinians. The PLO has used terrorist methods to try to achieve its goals. But it has also gained UN recognition as a legitimate organization representing the Palestinian people.

Fighting between the PLO and Israel continues. Although peace talks have sometimes led to successful negotiations, violence and politics have prevented any lasting peace agreement from being achieved.

would also include women fighting beside men, which, according to some strict interpretations of Islam, is immoral. And finally, the United States is widely hated in the Muslim world for its longstanding support of the state of Israel. Arabs and other Muslims see the Jewish nation as having unjustly taken land away from the Palestinians (Arabs had long lived in the area where Israel was founded).

PUBLIC RELATIONS

Saddam quickly realized that the world would not overlook the invasion of Kuwait as he had hoped. The United Nations Security Council condemned the invasion within 24 hours. A UN declaration demanded that Iraqi forces leave Kuwait immediately. On August 6, in an effort to put pressure on the Iraqis to leave Kuwait, the Security Council issued another resolution that banned almost all trade with Iraq. Slightly more than one week after the invasion, the Arab League dealt Iraq a serious blow. The league not only condemned the invasion but also agreed to send Arab soldiers to Saudi Arabia to protect that country's borders.

International reaction to Iraq's invasion was not all negative. Some Arabs were happy that Saddam had struck boldly at a friend of the United States, even though that friend was an Arab country. In the long run, they thought, Saddam's move would lead to a resurgence (reawakening) of Arab culture and political power. They admired Saddam's decisiveness and believed that Iraqi control of Kuwait would weaken Western influence in the Middle East.

Saddam increased his appeal among these Arabs by proclaiming himself a champion of the Palestinians. Saddam met with Palestinian leader Yasser Arafat two days after the invasion, as if to draw a connection between his actions and the Palestinian situation.

Iraq's government at first defended its invasion as an attempt to free Kuwaitis from an undemocratic and unstable government. Iraqi-controlled radio stations within Kuwait claimed that Kuwaitis themselves had risen up against the emir and that Iraqi troops were only supporting this revolution. Most governments around the world rejected this claim.

After a few days, Iraq's government offered a different reason for the invasion. Iraq started referring to Kuwait as the "Nineteenth Province" of Iraq. It declared that all Kuwaiti citizens were actually Iraqi citizens.

4 DESERT SHIELD

President George H. W. Bush knew that the United States could not drive Iraqi forces from Kuwait on its own. It would require a coalition, a group of nations acting together. Member nations might send soldiers, provide money, allow coalition planes to fly through their airspace, or even permit coalition troops or planes or rescue teams to be based within their territory.

An important piece of the coalition fell into place on August 8, 1990. After hearing an in-person plea from U.S. secretary of defense Dick Cheney, King Fahd announced that he had changed his mind. Troops of a U.S.-led coalition would be permitted to set up bases in Saudi Arabia, as long as the United States promised to withdraw its soldiers after Kuwait had been reclaimed.

Bush's team began planning. Military plans were drawn up under the direction of two prominent generals. One was Colin Powell, chairman of the Joint Chiefs of Staff (JCS)—a group that brings together the top commanders of the U.S. Army, Navy, Air Force, Marine Corps, and Coast Guard. The other was H. Norman Schwarzkopf, head of the U.S. Army's Central Command (CENTCOM) in Tampa, Florida. CENTCOM's planners named their operation Desert Shield.

Desert Shield had three main aims: to protect Saudi Arabia from an invasion by the Iraqi troops massed on the Saudi-Kuwaiti border; to build a force large enough to take Kuwait, if necessary; and to scare Iraq into withdrawing without a war. The first aim was the most urgent. If Iraq took Saudi Arabia as well as Kuwait, Saddam Hussein would control 40 percent of the world's known oil supplies.

WORKING THE PHONES

President Bush prided himself on reaching important agreements by picking up the telephone to talk to and persuade world leaders. His personal approach to building the coalition was effective with many countries, including some reluctant partners.

Great Britain needed no persuasion. The British prime minister, Margaret

U.S. president George H.W. Bush shakes hands with Britain's prime minister Margaret Thatcher. Thatcher promised Britain's support if the United States engaged in war against Iraq.

Thatcher, urged Bush to act quickly and promised Britain's support. Other traditional allies were a tougher sell. Both Egypt and Turkey were willing to publicly criticize Iraq, but they were reluctant to get involved in any war. Both feared great economic damage. Egypt, for example, depended heavily on money sent home by Egyptians working in Iraq and Kuwait. They would probably lose their jobs if Egypt joined the coalition. Bush promised to cancel billions of dollars of Egyptian debt to the United States, and Egypt agreed to join the coalition. Turkey agreed to join after Bush convinced Kuwait's emir to agree to pay Turkey up to $2 billion for any damage caused by the war.

The most remarkable cooperation came from the Soviet Union. The Soviets had once been Iraq's main arms supplier. But they refused to support Iraq since that would put them into a possible war with the United States. No one wanted to start a war between two superpowers like the United States and the Soviet Union.

A MASSIVE BUILDUP

Early in September, members of the U.S. Army's 82nd Airborne Division began arriving in Dhahran, Saudi Arabia. This small team could never have stopped an Iraqi invasion of eastern Saudi Arabia. Its main purpose was to show Iraq that an invasion of Saudi Arabia meant war with the United States. U.S. equipment began arriving through Saudi ports on the Gulf and on the Red Sea (on Saudi Arabia's western coast). Airfields at Dhahran and Riyadh took on a growing fleet of U.S. fighter jets and other aircraft.

FIGHTERS FROM VIRGINIA

Some of the first U.S. aircraft to arrive in Saudi Arabia were F-15 fighter planes that flew to Saudi Arabia from Langley, Virginia, in just 15 hours. These small aircraft could not hold enough fuel for a 15-hour flight, but they were able to refuel in the air by docking with refueling planes called tanker aircraft.

Conforming to Saudi Culture

Saudi Arabia is a strict, conservative Islamic country. To help ensure that the Americans operating in Saudi Arabia would not offend Islamic traditions, the U.S. soldiers stationed there operated under special rules. No alcohol was allowed on base. In most cases, women had to cover their arms and legs when they went out in public. Men and women could not publicly display physical affection toward each other. In addition, when off the U.S. military base, women sometimes had to wear the *abaya*, the long, black outer dress of Saudi women, and be accompanied by a man. Women, even female pilots, were not allowed to drive.

Ships steamed toward the Gulf region. Early in Desert Shield, the U.S. aircraft carrier (a kind of floating airport) USS *Eisenhower* sailed into the Red Sea. Another carrier, the USS *Independence,* entered the Gulf. Huge cargo ships called Maritime Prepositioning Ships—full of Marine Corps supplies, vehicles, and artillery—sailed north on the one-week journey from Diego Garcia to Saudi Arabia. Battleships and patrol boats, troop carriers and cargo ships all started heading to the Gulf from

their home ports in Southeast Asia, Georgia, and California. British, French, and Spanish supplies came in from bases throughout Europe.

Ten U.S. aircraft carriers and missile cruisers steam into the Red Sea to prepare for war against Iraq.

IRAQ STRENGTHENS ITS GRIP

Meanwhile, in Kuwait, Iraqi occupation troops tried to consolidate their control. All telephone service between Kuwait and the rest of the world was cut off. Saddam declared that no one could leave Kuwait or Iraq, and troops were sent to seal Kuwait's borders.

Many Kuwaitis had fled just after the invasion. Among the Kuwaiti citizens still in the country were resistance fighters. They staged hit-and-run attacks against Iraqi troops and conducted raids against Iraq's resources in Kuwait. Iraqi troops swiftly executed anyone suspected of helping the resistance and imprisoned other Kuwaitis for behaving suspiciously. Reports of rape and torture of Kuwaitis came out of the country at the time, and many of these were later proved to be true by investigators for human rights groups.

Palestinians were the largest group of foreign workers in Kuwait—about 400,000 in early August 1990. About 180,000 Palestinians remained in Kuwait through all or most of 1990. Some believed life would be better for them under Iraqi rule. Others joined the anti-Iraq resistance.

HUMAN SHIELDS

Foreign workers left Kuwait by the tens of thousands. Many traveled across the desert toward Saudi Arabia before Iraq could close the border. Some made it, but others were either turned back or arrested. Most people chose to stay where they were until their nations' embassies could fly them out. After a few weeks, Saddam's government allowed diplomats to arrange charter flights so Italians, Filipinos, Bangladeshis, and others could go back home.

This Kuwaiti home was totally destroyed by Iraqi soldiers during their occupation of Kuwait City.

A Nation of Foreigners

About 2.1 million people lived in Kuwait at the time of the 1990 invasion. More than half of them (about 62 percent) were foreign workers from at least 30 different countries. They were bank managers, engineers, teachers, construction laborers, and people from almost every other line of work. About 3,000 Americans were among them.

Foreign workers in Kuwait fell into two main categories, expatriates and *bidoun* (Arabic for "without"). Expatriates have a definite home country, to which they usually return after their work is done. In Kuwait, a stateless worker (usually an Arab) who is not a Kuwaiti citizen nor a citizen of any other country is called a bidoun.

U.S. and British families in Kuwait were not so lucky. Saddam declared that they had to stay. He called them "guests" of the Iraqi government. On August 23, he staged a televised meeting with their children, behaving like a kindly uncle. But the U.S. and British workers and their governments knew they were all prisoners. On August 28, Saddam said that women and children of all nationalities could leave if they wanted to, but British and American men had to stay. The men were later told to report to two hotels in Kuwait City. Those who obeyed were placed under house arrest in the hotels and later taken to Iraq. There they were moved to places such as power plants or water-treatment centers, which were likely targets if war erupted in Iraq. The prisoners were being used as "human shields" to keep coalition bombs away.

EYEWITNESS QUOTE: STATELESS

"It's all right for you. You have a country to go to. If we have to leave Kuwait, where do we go?"

—Mohammad, a Palestinian born in Kuwait

CHOOSING SIDES

Very few nations expressed support for Iraq during the final months of 1990. Iraq's friends included mostly small nations, such as Cuba and Yemen, that intensely disliked the United States. The PLO, which spoke for the Arabs of Palestine, also supported Iraq.

The only major nation to declare itself on Iraq's side was the Hashemite Kingdom of Jordan, Iraq's neighbor to the northwest. Its location between Iraq and Israel presented Jordan with many problems. (A joke at the time spoke of Jordan as being "between Iraq and a hard place.") On one hand, Jordan's King Hussein was generally pro-American, and George Bush considered the king a personal friend. The king's wife, Queen Noor, is an American. On the other hand, Jordan depended on Iraq for much of its trade, and it was close enough to be attacked if Saddam Hussein saw the kingdom as a source of trouble.

The coalition was made up of about forty countries, fifteen of which sent troops to the Middle East. By late 1990, troops from nine Arab nations—Bahrain, Egypt, Kuwait, Morocco, Oman, Qatar, Saudi Arabia, Syria, and the United Arab Emirates—were in northeastern Saudi Arabia under the overall command of General Schwarzkopf.

DESERT STORM
5 BEGINS

Facing the possibility of war against the coalition, Saddam tried to bargain. Throughout October and November 1990, Iraq offered to withdraw from Kuwait if certain conditions were met. On October 16, Saddam's government said Iraqi troops would leave most of Kuwait if Iraq could keep some Kuwaiti islands near the mouth of the Shatt al-Arab. Whether or not Saddam really expected to get the islands, his offers kept alive the hope that a peaceful end to the conflict could be found. He also allowed the American and British human shields to leave Iraq.

In the United States and elsewhere, people eagerly grasped at any hope for peace. They were very worried that a war to liberate Kuwait would cause massive destruction. In the past, Saddam's military had used chemical weapons against Iran and against Iraq's own Kurds. Iraq might very well do the same against coalition troops or even against civilian populations in Saudi Arabia or Israel. Antiwar demonstrations occurred in several U.S. cities, and many members of the U.S. Congress expressed concern about the dangers of marching against Iraq's armed forces.

Partly to limit Saddam's delaying tactics, the United Nations Security Council passed a resolution on November 29, 1990. The resolution stated that Iraq had to withdraw from Kuwait by January 15, 1991. If it failed to do so, members of the United Nations could use "all necessary means" to enforce earlier resolutions demanding a withdrawal. This resolution gave advance approval for military action by the coalition after January 15, 1991.

On January 9, 1991, U.S. secretary of state James Baker met with Iraq's foreign minister, Tariq Aziz, in Geneva, Switzerland, to deliver a message from President Bush for Saddam. The meeting's only result was to make peace seem less likely. Aziz refused to accept the letter. After the meeting, reporters asked the foreign minister whether Iraq might strike at Israel if war erupted. He said, "Yes. Absolutely yes."

By threatening Israel, Saddam knew that he could splinter the coalition. If Israel became involved, most of the Arab members of the coalition would drop out, which would badly weaken the coalition. For this reason, the United States had begged Israel to stay out of the war, and Israel had agreed.

On January 12, 1991, both the Senate and the House of Representatives voted to use U.S. troops to enforce the United Nations' resolution against Iraq's occupation of Kuwait. On January 16, Bush gave the order for the first phase of the war to begin. Desert Shield had turned into Desert Storm.

AN AIR BARRAGE

The operation began in the predawn darkness of January 17. In raids starting at about 1:30 A.M., U.S. Pave Low attack helicopters struck early-warning radar stations in remote parts of southern Iraq. These

---

EYEWITNESS QUOTE: TO WAR

"The mother of all battles has started. Satan Bush committed his crime."

—Saddam Hussein, referring to George H.W. Bush's decision to go to war against Iraq

---

attacks were followed by a massive air raid on Baghdad. The first strikes on the city were by Tomahawk cruise missiles fired from U.S. ships in the Red Sea and the Gulf. They devastated Iraqi command and control centers in the capital.

Cruise missiles can be fired from a long distance and are programmed to recognize hills, buildings, and other features. The missiles were used to disable many of Iraq's air defenses. Cruise missiles had never before been used in a real battle.

Following the cruse missile attacks were bombings by F-117 stealth fighter-bombers. Stealth fighters slipped in to destroy the very radar stations that were trying to track them.

THE FIRST COMPUTER WAR

The success of cruise missiles and other high-tech weapons showed that this was a totally new kind of war. The coalition's bombs guided by laser beams, preprogrammed missiles, pinpoint positioning using satellites circling the earth, and other technology allowed for shorter battles, more precise bombing, and less human exposure to enemy fire. In fact, the 1991 Gulf War is sometimes called "the first Computer War."

The combination of cruise missile attacks, stealth fighter operations, and helicopter sweeps proved devastating for Iraq's air defenses. Many radar sites and command centers were destroyed. Those that still functioned were unable to detect most of the aircraft attacking them.

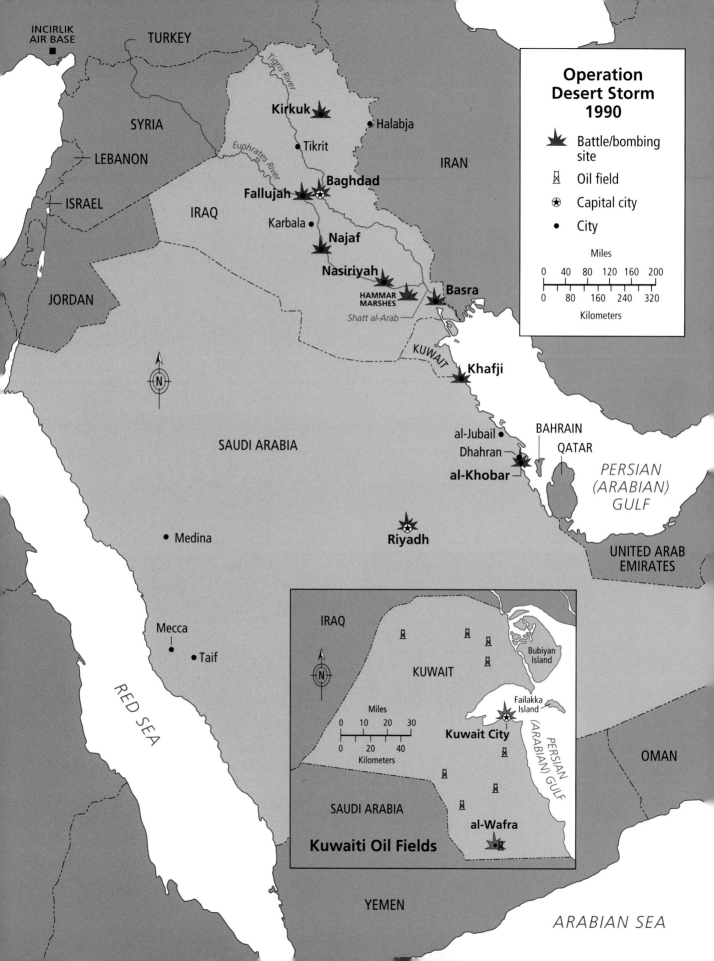

Stealth Fighter-Bombers

Stealth aircraft, such as the F-117 stealth fighter-bomber *(right)*, are built to avoid being tracked by radar. When radar signals strike a stealth aircraft, a special exterior coating and the plane's odd shape absorb some of the signals and scatter others in various directions. The radar waves do not bounce back to a receiver as they would if striking an ordinary fighter jet.

After cruise missiles and stealth craft severely damaged Iraq's defenses, other U.S., British, and French fighters and bombers flew in to hit targets other than Baghdad. Almost all of Iraq's 36 bridges over the Tigris and Euphrates rivers were destroyed or damaged to stop the flow of supplies through the country. About 2,000 sorties (trips by individual aircraft) were flown against Iraq on the first day of battle. Many of the attacking aircraft were equipped with "smart bombs," laser-guided explosives that could strike targets with an accuracy never before seen in real combat.

This bridge over the Euphrates River in Nasiriyah, Iraq, was destroyed by coalition air strikes. By taking out bridges, the coalition hoped to cripple Iraqi transportation of supplies.

WOMEN

During the Persian Gulf and Iraqi wars, women played a far greater role in the U.S. military than they ever had before. More than 40,000 women from the regular and reserve forces went on active duty in the Gulf region. They were assigned a variety of duties. Some of these had previously been assigned only to men. Women served also in more traditional roles as nurses and communications controllers.

Although there were many new roles for women in the military, about one in seven combat positions were still restricted to men. Women could not be fighter pilots, which is considered a combat role. But women did serve as helicopter pilots, army surgeons, intelligence officers, and military police, as well as in a wide variety of other jobs. (Unlike female U.S. soldiers, women in Iraq were allowed to enter combat. In contrast to the practice in some conservative Islamic countries such as Iran, Iraqi women are well educated, can bear arms, and do not have to cover their faces.)

Women served in every branch of the U.S. military. Unlike in earlier wars, noncombatants (medical, communications, and supply personnel, for example) serving in the Gulf region received combat training because they carried weapons. In many instances, noncombatants (including women) did in fact participate in combat.

American women in Iraq served bravely. Women dropped from planes as paratroopers, performed lifesaving surgery as military doctors, and fought to defend U.S. troops when fired upon. Some, like Rhonda Cornum, the first American woman captured in Iraq, became prisoners of war. Others, including 16 women who died during Desert Storm, gave their lives for their country.

Private First Class Lori Piestewa's army maintenance unit was ambushed in Iraq on March 23, 2003, while she was driving the truck that Private First Class Jessica Lynch, among other soldiers, was riding. Piestewa pulled out her gun and fought bravely to defend herself and her companions. She was one of nine who died in the ambush and the first Native American woman to die fighting for the United States. Lynch was taken prisoner and was later welcomed as a hero when she returned to the United States.

MINORITY SOLDIERS IN THE GULF WAR

The U.S. forces stationed in the Gulf in 1990–1991 and again in the early 2000s were made up of a far more mixed population that ever before. Nearly half of the troops were minorities or women. Two of the largest minority groups were African Americans and Hispanics, but people from a wide range of races and backgrounds were represented.

African Americans African Americans made up between 20 and 30 percent of the troops active in the Gulf War. Fewer than 12 percent of all Americans are of African descent. The number of African American officers remained low compared to total troop numbers. General Colin Powell, chairman of the Joint Chiefs of Staff and one of the leaders of the U.S. military during Desert Shield and Desert Storm, is African American.

Hispanics Many Hispanic soldiers served in the Gulf in 1991, but a far greater number served in 2003. Many Latino men and women joined the armed forces for an opportunity to gain employment skills, a job, and an education.

"Green Card Soldiers" A number of permanent residents of the United States, who were not citizens, also volunteered and fought in Iraq in the 2003 war. More than 30,000 noncitizen residents, who held cards (commonly referred to as green cards) that made them legal residents of the United States, were on active duty. They were known as "green card soldiers." In 2002 President George W. Bush had signed an order to grant citizenship more quickly to these soldiers. More than 10,000 green card soldiers were in the reserves in 2003. Two marines, Lance Corporal Jose Gutierrez and Corporal Jose Garibay, were granted citizenship after they had been killed as the United States moved into southern Iraq in March 2003.

Muslims The first Muslim chaplain (minister), Abdul-Rasheed Muhammad, was appointed to the U.S. military in 1993. By that time, more that 2,500 Muslims were serving in the U.S. armed forces. By 2003 more than 4,000 of the members of the U.S. military were Muslims. Many of these people have served the United States in Iraq.

Native Americans Native Americans have always been important to the U.S. military. Based on the size of the Native American population compared to the country as a whole, more Native Americans join the military than any other ethnic group. Until recently, nearly all of these recruits were men. In 2003, however, more than 4,000 Native American women were serving in the U.S. military.

One videotape released by the U.S. Department of Defense showed a laser-targeted smart bomb missile heading toward a building. The bomb "found" a vent opening in the roof and flew inside before a cloud of smoke, which indicated an explosion, appeared.

Within a day, the coalition had shown it was clearly superior in the skies over Kuwait and Iraq. But superiority did not mean total control. Iraqi fighters downed ten coalition planes (including six from the United States) in the first two days of combat.

SCUD MISSILES

Iraq had a large supply of Scud missiles, which it had bought from the Soviet Union. Scuds are large, ground-launched missiles. They are slow and easy for radar to detect, and they have a range of up to 400 miles. Scuds could easily reach Israel's cities from launchers in far western Iraq or hit Saudi cities such as Dhahran and Riyadh from launchers in southern Iraq. Iraq had also developed ways to move Scud launchers from place to place and to hide them from coalition spy planes and satellites. Iraq had warheads (tips) for these missiles that contained chemical weapons. If they used these warheads, they could cause a huge number of deaths with just one accurate strike.

From January 17 to February 24, Iraq fired Scuds at Israel, Saudi Arabia, and Bahrain. A total of 39 Scuds hit Israel in a five-week period. Dozens of Israelis were injured, but only one death was directly caused by a missile attack. Air-raid sirens sent panicked Israelis grabbing for gas masks in case one of the missiles contained a chemical or poison gas. None did. Many Scuds missed their targets—including one aimed at an Israeli nuclear power plant. The attacks failed to draw Israel into the conflict.

Scud attacks on Saudi Arabia were generally less successful because the United States had antimissile equipment in place from the start. (Such equipment was not shipped to Israel until after the Scud attacks had been going on for about a

U.S. soldiers examine the wreckage of an Iraqi Scud missile that was shot down by a Patriot missile over Saudi Arabia.

week.) A U.S. missile called the Patriot intercepted many Scuds headed for Dhahran and Riyadh, in Saudi Arabia, but the Patriot defenses did not always work. One Scud managed to get through and hit Riyadh. Even Scuds that were hit by Patriot missiles could be destructive if they fell onto populated areas after being hit.

ENVIRONMENTAL DAMAGE

As the coalition overwhelmed his troops, Saddam decided to do as much damage as possible to Kuwait before coalition forces pushed them out. On January 22, Saddam ordered Iraqi troops to begin destroying Kuwait's oil resources. They set oil wells on fire, burning Kuwait's precious oil fields and sending black plumes of smoke into the air. Iraqi soldiers also deliberately opened a Kuwaiti oil pipeline (which carries oil to tankers docked at harbors) to spill oil into the Gulf. The flow of oil into the Gulf continued for five days, until U.S. Air Force planes bombed the pipeline farther inland. The oil then spilled out onto the barren sands instead of into the water. The five-day spill was estimated by some organizations as the largest ever in the world. The resulting slick of oil devastated coral reefs and choked sea life throughout the northern Gulf. As the slick moved south, teams of engineers scrambled, in the middle of a war zone, to contain it before it could reach water desalination plants at al-Jubail in Saudi Arabia. These plants produce drinkable water for the Saudis by removing salt from seawater.

THE IRAQI POINT OF VIEW

In August 1990, Iraq was deeply in debt and trying to rebuild after the Iran-Iraq War. Still, Iraq had one of the most powerful armies in the region. Saddam's government told the Iraqi people that Kuwait was stealing Iraqi oil, that Kuwait was causing Iraq's money problems by keeping oil prices low, and that Kuwait was really a part of Iraq. Saddam also told Iraqis that, with such a powerful army, Iraq should be a major leader in the Middle East. This led to public support in Iraq for an invasion of Kuwait. But after the Iran-Iraq War, most Iraqis did not want to face another long war. They were afraid that occupying Kuwait would be just that.

In addition, suspicion was growing about the United States. The Cold War (1945–1991) was winding down, and the Soviet Union was not considered a major threat to the United States anymore. Iraqis thought that if the United States was not concentrating on the Soviet Union, it would use its power and money to control other countries. Iraqi people, influenced by government propaganda (information given out by the government to support the government's plans), began to feel that the United States was planning to destroy Iraq. This idea was expressed by Foreign Minister Tariq Aziz: "Iraq was designated by George Bush for destruction, with or without Kuwait. Inside Kuwait or outside Kuwait. Before the 2nd of August or after the 2nd of August [1991]."

Some Iraqis, particularly in the military, believed in the powerful Iraq promoted by Saddam. Plenty more did as they were told out of fear. An end to Saddam's rule of terror might have been welcomed in 1991, if the United States had occupied Baghdad and ousted Saddam.

THE FIGHTING CONTINUES

The coalition had setbacks as well as successes in the air war. On February 13, U.S. bombers targeted a building in Baghdad thought to hold Iraqi military personnel. The destruction of this building, which Iraq claimed was an air-raid shelter, killed about 400 Iraqi civilians. U.S. officers said that even though civilians were inside, it was a military installation. And even smart bombs went astray. An incorrectly targeted smart-bomb attack by British jets killed 130 civilians near the town of Fallujah.

While the air war continued, so did the bombing from warships in the Gulf. Dodging Iraqi mines (explosives floating in the water), coalition ships sailed close to Kuwait and Iraq. They bombarded areas where Iraqi troops were digging in to prepare for a ground assault by the coalition— a battle that the United States and its allies did not really want.

THE GROUND WAR

6

A ground war—a massive land invasion of coalition troops, tanks, and other vehicles—against the Iraqis in Kuwait would be a lot riskier than the air war. In ground combat, Iraq had natural advantages. Between 300,000 and 500,000 regular Iraqi troops were in or near Kuwait. More than 1 million other young men in Iraq could quickly be drafted into the war if necessary.

As the defender in the upcoming battle for Kuwait, Iraq also had advantages. It could strengthen its tank positions, store up supplies, set up ambushes (shooting from secret cover), and lay traps and minefields (explosives buried in the ground set to go off when stepped on). The coalition

force was large—about 740,000 troops (about 500,000 Americans) by mid-February—but leaders worried that it was not large enough. Military planners estimate that an attacking force on the ground usually has to be three times as large as a defending force in order to overcome the defenders' advantages.

The technology gap between Iraqi forces and coalition forces on the ground was narrower than in the air. Iraq's tanks and heavy weapons were modern and dangerous. Most feared of all were Iraq's chemical and biological weapons. Unlike a pilot in a jet, a division of soldiers on the ground is an easy target for poison gas or a spray of germs. One low-tech missile with a poisonous warhead could spread panic and death through the coalition forces.

The first ground battles of the war were fought in extreme northern Saudi Arabia. On January 29, 1991, Iraqi troops crossed the border into the Saudi desert south of the Kuwaiti town of al-Wafra. U.S. Marines supported by fighter jets drove them out. The same day, Iraqis succeeded in occupying a town called Khafji, from which all the residents had fled earlier. The Iraqis held the town for about a day and a half until Saudi and Qatari soldiers defeated them in house-to-house fighting.

EYEWITNESS QUOTE:
IRAQI SOLDIER

"My hatred [for Americans and the British] increased since they bombed civilians and buildings where my family is living nearby. Because I know nothing of my family my grudge against them is bigger. I wish they started their ground war, whatever the consequences might be."

—from the diary of an Iraqi soldier in Kuwait City

These two battles were important for the coalition, but they also pointed up a grave danger. In an incident south of al-Wafra, seven marines were killed by "friendly fire" (coalition troops accidentally attacking or firing on other coalition troops) when a U.S. jet bombed their truck. A top U.S. commander, Lieutenant General Thomas Kelly said, "Once a bullet leaves a gun, it has no friends."

OIL WELL FIRES

As the coalition moved into a ground war, Iraq continued working to destroy Kuwait's oil industry. Explosives placed at more than 1,000 oil wells were set off.

Flames and black smoke spew from Kuwaiti oil wells. The fires were set by retreating Iraqi troops.

President Bush *(far right)* meets with his advisers, including Colin Powell *(second from left)*, on February 21, 1991, to discuss the U.S. response to a Soviet peace plan with Iraq.

Black smoke from the oil well fires blew from Kuwait over eastern Saudi Arabia, Bahrain, Qatar, and parts of Iran. Wherever the smoke was thickest, a black, greasy soot collected on outdoor surfaces. President Bush deplored Iraq's tactics and spoke out publicly against them.

Then on February 15, Iraq's government surprised the coalition by saying it was ready to listen to the UN's withdrawal demands. On February 21, 1991, Soviet president Gorbachev, who had met earlier with Iraqi leaders in an effort to avoid a war, announced that Iraq intended to withdraw fully from Kuwait within three weeks. President Bush saw this as yet another delaying tactic. He told the Iraqis to start withdrawing from Kuwait by February 23 and finish within a week or risk a ground attack in Iraq.

NO EYES IN THE AIR

Iraq had little way of knowing where such an attack might come from. Because coalition aircraft dominated the skies, the Iraqis could not send spy planes to survey the forces massing in northern Saudi Arabia. Iraq's knowledge about coalition ships in the Gulf was a little better, thanks to reports from Iraqi agents in small patrol boats and onshore observers with binoculars.

> ### EYEWITNESS QUOTE: CONSCIENCE
>
> "Someone once asked, 'What is the difference between me and Saddam Hussein?' The answer is, 'I have a conscience and he doesn't.'"
>
> —General Norman Schwarzkopf, 1991

The Iraqis probably thought the coalition would first attack Kuwaiti islands, such as Failakka and Bubiyan, just off the coast of Kuwait. The coalition encouraged the Iraqis to believe that a sea attack was coming by practicing landings along the Saudi coast and by bombing the islands.

The real strength of the coalition force, however, was concentrated along a 300-mile stretch of Saudi Arabia's borders with Kuwait and Iraq. The Iraqis were sure troops would be placed along the Saudi-Kuwait part of the border. So Saddam divided his forces between the border and the coast. Iraqi soldiers were dug in along the 125-mile-long border between the two countries. What they did not seem to expect was the coalition buildup 200 miles to the west, far from Kuwait.

GOING IN

Bush's deadline of February 23 passed without any sign of an Iraqi withdrawal. Coalition forces began clearing an assault route into Iraq by bombing minefields, sending bulldozers through berms (long mounds) of sand built by the Iraqis, and setting fire to trenches the Iraqis had filled with oil. The Iraqi plan had been to light this oil later to confuse advancing troops. The coalition simply burned it all off before it could be used against them.

The final phase of the war for Kuwait began early on a Sunday morning, February 24, 1991. Some coalition troops, mostly combined forces from the United States and Arab countries, pushed directly into Kuwait. Other forces, mostly U.S., British, and French, entered southwestern Iraq. These forces in the southwest would

U.S. Marines in Saudi Arabia return to their camp following a training exercise in preparation for Operation Desert Storm.

A convoy of coalition troops makes its way into the desert of Iraq from Saudi Arabia in 1991.

try to get behind Iraq's units in Kuwait, cutting off their retreat. General Schwarzkopf, during military planning sessions, sometimes referred to this move as a "left hook" because, on a map, the troop movement resembles a boxer's left hand coming across to strike a blow.

Part of the left-hook forces flew by helicopter about 80 miles into Iraq, where they set up Forward Operations Base Cobra. This base gave them a place from which to strike eastward to the Euphrates River valley. They were only about 150 miles southwest of Baghdad, yet they had arrived without taking any enemy fire.

The troops moving directly into Kuwait had rougher travel. They had to go over or through sand berms, trenches, and minefields put up by the Iraqis. When they came to a minefield that had not first been cleared by a bombing run, they used a tank-mounted MICLIC (Mine-Clearing Line Charge) to blast a path through it. The MICLIC was a 100-yard-long tube full of explosives. After the tube was flung out into a minefield, the tube blew up and detonated the mines near it. The forces advanced through the open lane and then used another MICLIC to clear more land in front of them.

HUMMERS

A new kind of military vehicle saw its first action during the 1991 Gulf War—the Humvee. This large, powerful jeeplike vehicle was used to transport troops and supplies over rough territory. Some Americans found the rugged vehicles attractive. So General Motors—the maker of the Humvee—produced a nonmilitary model, the Hummer.

FAST FACT

SOLDIERS AND THEIR UNIFORMS

U.S. SOLDIERS U.S. soldiers in the Persian Gulf and Iraqi wars of 1991 and 2003 were volunteers, either full-time recruits or reservists. They were generally older, better trained, and better educated than soldiers in earlier American wars. But at the time of the Gulf War, not many had experienced actual combat conditions.

Nearly all U.S. soldiers had completed high school, and a majority expected to graduate from college, if they had not already. Most of the high-ranking officers in the army had master's degrees. In addition, the complicated technology of modern warfare requires extensive training of all recruits, regardless of rank.

Because the soldiers were older and more of them were reservists, many left husbands, wives, and children behind when they went to the Gulf. They were facing a new kind of battle for the United States—they not only had to fight in a harsh desert climate, but they also had to be prepared for an enemy with chemical and possibly biological and nuclear weapons. On the eve of battle in 2003, U.S. Army captain Clint Esarey dictated onto a tape to be delivered to his wife, "If I don't make it back, I want to be buried in my military uniform. I'm a soldier. It's my life. The uniform is part of me."

American Uniforms U.S. soldiers' uniforms and equipment varied depending on their branch in the military and their assignment. However, a typical soldier *(right)* wore an olive or tan camouflage-pattern shirt and pants, combat boots, a Kevlar helmet (Kevlar is a bulletproof material), and a Kevlar vest. Among the items in the 60 pounds-plus of equipment that soldiers in both wars carried were:

Weapons
- an M-16 rifle
- a 9-millimeter pistol
- a fighting knife
- ammunition

Necessities for Desert Warfare
- sunscreen and lip balm
- sunglasses
- infrared night-vision goggles for fighting at night, when it is cooler
- two one-quart canteens of water
- sleeping bags and clothing

Biological, Chemical, and Nuclear Precautions
- gas mask
- suits to provide protection from toxic gases, microbes (germs), and radioactive fallout (since these suits could become hot in the desert sun, some were even equipped with personal cooling systems)
- kits containing antidotes in case of nerve gas exposure

IRAQI SOLDIERS

The Iraqi army had two regular branches, the Republican Guard and the regular army. The Republican Guard had originally been a select group of palace guards whom Saddam had chosen from the area surrounding his home in Tikrit. During the Iran-Iraq War, this group had been expanded. By the beginning of Operation Desert Storm, the Republican Guard had more

than 100,000 specially trained and equipped soldiers. The Republican Guards were proud, motivated, well equipped, and disciplined. They had had extensive training. Many were experienced veterans, who had fought in the Iran-Iraq War. Regular army soldiers appeared to coalition soldiers to only obey orders out of fear of their superior officers.

In addition to these two military branches, civilian volunteers fought as part of the People's Army. These volunteers received less training than the regular army and were not very effective against U.S. forces.

Iraqi Uniforms Iraqi soldiers *(below)* wore olive drab shirts and pants and boots or high-top shoes. They also wore olive drab caps or helmets. Some Muslim women in the People's Army wore black scarves over their heads, but most women wore the same caps as the men, with their hair tied back tightly. Soldiers often carried Iraqi or Russian assault rifles and Iraqi pistols. Iraqi soldiers also carried necessities such as water, food, and sleeping bags. In some cases, Iraqi soldiers had gas masks with a special hose for attaching a canteen so that the soldier could drink water even in an area where chemical weapons were being used.

During Operation Desert Storm, coalition forces encountered thousands of Iraqi soldiers who preferred to surrender rather than put up a fight.

Most of the U.S. troops on the ground either wore or carried chemical-warfare suits. These protective outfits looked something like space suits. They were sealed to keep out chemicals or germs and were very hot and very heavy.

SURRENDER AND RESISTANCE

At first, the Iraqi forces didn't put up much of a fight. As coalition troops advanced, most of the surviving Iraqi soldiers either surrendered or retreated northward. About 10,000 Iraqis surrendered the first day. Over the four-day span of the ground war, at least 58,000 soldiers had surrendered. Coalition troops suddenly had a prisoner-of-war problem, with tens of thousands of tired, hungry, and defeated Iraqi soldiers to take care of.

EYEWITNESS QUOTE:
KUWAIT CITY PULLOUT

"Iraqis are killing civilians as they pull out of Kuwait City, probably so as not to leave witnesses of the atrocities. Lots of executions, decapitations, rapes."

—Phillip Thompson, U.S. Marine, journal entry, February 26, 1991

The heaviest death toll for coalition troops came from an Iraqi attack on the evening of February 25. It occurred 200 miles away from Kuwait. A Scud missile approaching Dhahran, Saudi Arabia, was detected on radar and hit by a Patriot missile. The disabled Scud fell on a barracks (housing area) for U.S. soldiers in al-Khobar, just outside Dhahran. Twenty-eight soldiers were killed.

The toughest battles of the ground war came when U.S. forces ran into divisions of Iraq's Republican Guard. These units of Iraq's army were the best-trained, best-equipped, and most loyal of Saddam's forces. They were stationed deep in Kuwait and in southern Iraq so they wouldn't have to absorb the first fire of a ground attack. From a more protected position, they were supposed to move up and eliminate any coalition troops who managed to break through Iraq's first lines of defense.

Perhaps the longest battle of the ground war started on February 26. U.S. Army forces pushing east as part of the "left hook" maneuver encountered part of a division of the Republican Guard. The Guard fought hard for more than a day before being defeated. A tough, though shorter, battle took place near the Kuwait City International Airport on February 26, as coalition forces took control of the airport.

A TURKEY SHOOT

Arab and U.S. troops closed in on Kuwait City on February 25 and 26. A separate group of U.S. Marines drove northward just west of the city. They took up positions on some high ground known as Mutlah Ridge. This put them beside a highway that ran from the Kuwait City metropolitan area northward to Basra, Iraq's second-largest city.

This road came to be known as the "Highway of Death." When Iraqi troops fled Kuwait City—often in civilian cars and trucks—the marines on Mutlah Ridge attacked. Coalition aircraft flew overhead and destroyed vehicles at the head of the line of traffic. Ruined Iraqi tanks and personnel carriers made the road impassable and created a huge traffic jam. The fleeing Iraqi soldiers caught in this jam were easy targets for the coalition's fighter jets and helicopter gunships.

Iraqi forces abandoned Kuwait City by the end of the day on February 26. The

This highway, which leads from Kuwait City, Kuwait, to Basra, Iraq, became littered with bombed vehicles and the bodies of Iraqi soldiers as coalition troops tried to stop the retreat of Iraqi forces in February 1991. The highway became known as the "Highway of Death."

Iraqi occupation of Kuwait was over. The remaining battles of the war took place when coalition troops caught up with fleeing Iraqis, and the Iraqis fought to cover their retreat. Coalition troops in southern Iraq had advanced to the Euphrates and were attacking other parts of Iraq by air. No Arab troops were sent this far north so as to avoid creating the impression of an invasion of one Arab country by other Arab nations. U.S. and British forces took the lead in this pursuit, attacking from the air with such ease that the press started calling it a "turkey shoot," referring to the ease with which hunters are able to spot and kill wild turkeys. U.S. commanders began worrying that it looked cruel.

Nevertheless, the coalition failed to cut off this retreat completely. Iraqi forces still made their way to Basra across some bridges that spanned the Basra Canal. Others crossed the marshes of southern Iraq and reached the Euphrates River.

About half of the Republican Guard escaped back to Iraq.

Saddam Hussein's government in Baghdad was battered but defiant. It kept broadcasting reports of great Iraqi victories, but the conflict was just about over. Coalition troops were advancing with ease.

A TOUGH DECISION

At this point, President Bush faced a difficult decision. Coalition troops might be able to keep going, take Baghdad, and force Saddam from power. Or they could stay in southern Iraq, further weaken Saddam's defenses, and encourage various Iraqi groups to overthrow Saddam.

Generals Powell and Schwarzkopf argued that the goal of Desert Storm had been achieved. Kuwait had been liberated. To go further would look like aggression and might anger some coalition members. Bush agreed. The coalition advance stopped where it was at 8:00 in the morn-

THE HOME FRONT

As U.S. troops began to be sent to Saudi Arabia in the fall of 1990 to defend Saudi Arabia and to free Kuwait, yellow ribbons—symbols of support for U.S. troops stationed abroad—sprouted up all over the country. Fewer than half of Americans had favored going to war in the Gulf before January 15, 1991. But after the Gulf War began, about three-quarters of Americans believed that President Bush had done the right thing. The president's approval ratings soared.

This popular support for military action was not universal. Around the country, protesters carried signs demanding "No blood for oil!" Some Americans felt that the United States went to war only to protect Kuwait's oil supply. Many thought that the United States had no reason to sacrifice U.S. lives in a fight between foreign countries. However, most were pleased by the speed with which the war was conducted and the low number of U.S. casualties, even if they did not agree with the war itself.

Gulf War Syndrome

Medical professionals monitored the health of Gulf War veterans after they returned home. Many of the soldiers who had served in the war had been exposed to a variety of toxic chemicals. Exposure occurred from many sources: the smoke of the Kuwaiti oil fires, pesticides used by coalition forces to control rodents and flies, vaccinations the soldiers had received against Iraqi biological weapons, smoke and dust from the destruction of Iraqi weapons sites, and the dust that is produced after depleted uranium weapons (used by coalition forces) are fired. Many of the veterans

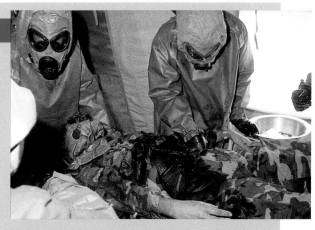

Doctors decontaminate a coalition patient before removing his suit in case he had been exposed to chemical or biological weapons.

suffered from symptoms such as stomach and lung problems, pain, fatigue, and memory loss. These symptoms became known as the Gulf War Syndrome. It is still not clear if the syndrome is directly related to the exposure to toxic chemicals or to other causes.

ing (Iraqi time) on February 28, 1991. Bush ordered the cease-fire to begin at this hour so the ground war would end exactly 100 hours after it had started.

THE CASUALTIES OF WAR

Except for one large battle between the U.S. Army and some retreating Iraqis near the Hammar Causeway (through the Hammar Marshes just west of Basra) on March 2, the cease-fire held. Altogether about 30,000 Iraqi soldiers and civilians had been killed during the air war and ground war combined. About 60,000 had been taken prisoner. About half of the Republican Guard was eliminated, but half of them survived. In all, 146 Americans had been killed, about one-fifth of those by friendly fire. The coalition as a whole suffered fewer than 200 deaths in battle. Iraq

held about 41 U.S. and British prisoners of war and about 2,100 Kuwaitis.

It looked as if Iraq had not used any chemical or biological weapons during the conflict, although coalition investigators continued for many months taking samples of air, soil, and water to search for signs of them. It was hard to believe that Iraq would not employ its most feared weapons. The hard-to-handle materials may have been stored far from the front lines in order to prevent accidents. The quick pace of the war may have kept them from being brought forward. It's also possible that Iraqi commanders could not call the weapons into use because communications had been interrupted. Perhaps Saddam felt that a chemical attack would lead to a full invasion of Iraq and the destruction of his regime.

THE WAR
7 GOES COLD

On March 2, 1991, the United Nations Security Council passed a resolution. It ordered Iraq to give up any claims to Kuwait, agree to pay for damages to that country, return coalition prisoners of war (POWs), and accept other limits on its military might. These included destroying all existing weapons of mass destruction and allowing teams of UN inspectors to oversee this process. It also included a ban on missiles that could fly farther than 93 miles, a rule meant to keep Iraqi Scuds from threatening Israel and Saudi Arabia again.

The next day, a meeting between the United States and Iraq was held at Safwan Airfield, in the Iraqi desert. General Schwarzkopf met with Iraqi lieutenant general Sultan Hashim Ahmad to work out the details of separating their forces. U.S. forces would be allowed to remain in the Gulf region, but not within the internationally recognized boundaries of Kuwait. U.S. forces remained in Saudi Arabia until mid-2003 to defend Saudi Arabia and Kuwait and to maintain Patriot missile shields to aid in this defense.

As the victor, Schwarzkopf was in a position to demand almost anything from Iraq. Instead, he went easy on the Iraqis in a couple of key areas. For one thing, he promised that coalition ground troops would leave Iraqi territory as soon as possible. Many observers thought the United States should stay in southern Iraq to make sure Saddam kept to his agreements. For another, although Schwarzkopf banned Iraqi airplanes from flying over much of southern Iraq, he allowed helicopters—even helicopter gunships—to fly there.

THE SHIITE UPRISING

Over the next few days, coalition troops slowly began withdrawing from southern Iraq. Meanwhile, Shiites in the area held anti-Saddam demonstrations, even claiming they were no longer under Saddam's rule. They had been encouraged by the speeches President Bush had given at the war's end, in which he suggested that the Iraqi people should overthrow Saddam. The Shiites probably expected

EYEWITNESS QUOTE:
WHERE'S BUSH?

"Bush told us to revolt against Saddam. We revolt against Saddam. But where is Bush? Where is he?"

—Shiite Iraqi recorded by U.S. general Bernard E. Trainor, 1991

U.S. troops to assist them if they started a rebellion.

A few days after the Safwan meeting, the Iraqi army began using helicopter gunships to hit Basra, Najaf, Nasiriyah, and other places where Shiites were rebelling. Refugees fled south toward the withdrawing U.S. forces in hopes of finding protection. Refugee camps sprang up wherever a coalition force remained.

Although unhappy that Saddam was still in power and concerned about the Shiite and refugee situations, Bush did not want to risk the military actions necessary to remove him. He also knew his Arab allies would not accept a U.S. invasion of Iraq to remove Saddam. In the end, the

Iraqi soldiers pose outside a destroyed mosque in Karbala, where Iraqi troops quelled a Shiite rebellion in March 1991.

Bush administration decided to complete the withdrawal of U.S. troops, call the 100-hour war a victory, and leave Iraqi internal affairs alone.

SADDAM STRIKES THE KURDS AND THE MARSH ARABS

Saddam portrayed his survival as victory. Official Iraqi statements about the mother of all battles claimed Iraq had won. Saddam ordered a huge new mosque built in Baghdad and named it the Mother of All Battles Mosque. The minarets (towers) of the mosque were built to look like Scud missiles.

Because Saddam remained in power with at least half of his Republican Guard intact, the Gulf War became a 12-year cold war (hostilities and mistrust that fall short of military action) between Iraq and the West that occasionally flared up into crisis.

As part of the March 2 resolution, inspectors from the United Nations searched Iraq for chemical, biological, and nuclear weapons and destroyed whatever they uncovered. When Saddam didn't cooperate and live up to the cease-fire commitments, the UN set up and maintained economic sanctions. These sanctions prevented Iraq from importing almost anything, including basic items such as food and medicine.

The Kurds of northern Iraq also rebelled in March 1991. They hoped to break away from Iraq and establish their own country. Saddam's military responded with air strikes that forced more than one million Kurds to flee for their lives to Turkey and Iran. The UN demanded that Iraq stop striking at the Kurds. The United States, France, and Great Britain decided to set up a zone of protection for them. They

Kurdish rebels defend their positions against Iraqi fire in March 1991.

Marsh Arabs, Shiite Muslims who make their living in the marshes of the Shatt al-Arab, suffered greatly after Iraq cracked down on the rebels and destroyed their way of life by draining marshes.

declared a no-fly zone in northern Iraq. The United States and its allies began patrolling the zone with fighter-bombers based on aircraft carriers at sea, in Saudi Arabia, and at the Incirlik air base in southern Turkey. They declared that any Iraqi aircraft flying in the zone would be shot down. Because the Kurdish region is mountainous and relatively far from Baghdad, the United States and its allies were able to create a zone of relative peace.

The northern no-fly zone worked so well that in 1993, the United States and Britain decide to set up a similar zone in the south to protect Iraqi Shiites. Iraqi aircraft were banned from the southernmost part of Iraq. This zone was less effective. Although the no-fly zone prevented Baghdad from attacking the south by air, ground forces continued assaults on minority peoples in that region.

Among the hardest hit were the Marsh Arabs, a group of rural Shiites who lived in a vast maze of freshwater wetlands west of the Shatt al-Arab. Their lifestyle in the marsh environment included wetland agriculture, fishing, and making round boats of tightly woven reeds. To punish the rebellious Marsh Arabs, the Iraq government destroyed their homeland. Baghdad's engineers drained the marshes and made the land almost useless. Their homeland marshes were turned into a salt-caked plain. Before the war, the Marsh Arabs probably numbered about 500,000. Ten years later, only a few thousand were still living in the area. The rest had fled to Iran or spread out to other parts of Iraq.

ASSASSINATION ATTEMPTS AND SUCCESSES

In November 1992, Bill Clinton defeated George H. W. Bush in the U.S. presidential elections. The next year, former president Bush traveled to Kuwait in April to celebrate the second anniversary of the liberation of Kuwait. A car packed with 175 pounds of explosives was discovered before it could be parked along the road Bush was to travel. Later investigations found strong evidence that the Iraq Intelligence Service was responsible for this assassination attempt. U.S. president Bill Clinton ordered a missile attack in

Family Matters

Saddam's family drew attention in the 1990s. His elder son, Uday, was appointed to several leadership positions. He displayed a shocking ruthlessness. For example, as the head of Iraq's national sports organization, he reportedly tortured members of the national soccer team if they did not play well. Uday made many enemies. Someone sprayed his car with rifle fire in December 1996, killing his bodyguards. Uday was gravely injured but recovered.

In 1995 two of Saddam's sons-in-law fled with their wives (Saddam's daughters) to Jordan. They spoke out for the removal of Saddam from power. Somehow, they were talked into returning to Iraq in February 1996, and Saddam had his daughters' husbands killed.

Saddam *(center)* and his sons Uday *(left)* and Qusay *(right)*

retaliation. In June a U.S. naval ship in the Gulf fired 23 cruise missiles to hit the headquarters of the Iraqi Intelligence Service in Baghdad.

Another crisis occurred when, in 1996, Saddam's government took sides in a conflict between two Kurdish political parties (the PUK and the KDP). Saddam sent about 40,000 soldiers to the north in support of one of the parties. The United States objected because these troops were within the protected area established in 1991.

The U.S. military fired two cruise missiles into southern Iraq, but there was little else the United States could do. The divisions among Kurdish politicians became less violent a few months later, after Iraq eventually moved its troops out. But the two main Kurdish parties continued to compete for various positions of power.

SYMPATHY FOR SADDAM

In the mid-1990s, many countries began to feel that the economic sanctions against Iraq, in place since 1991, were too strict. Russia, France, and Germany favored easing the sanctions. These countries felt that the sanctions were hurting innocent Iraqis more than they were hurting the Iraqi government. In 1996 Saddam agreed to an arrangement proposed by the United Nations called the oil-for-food program. With this program, the Iraqi government could sell a limited amount of oil to pay for food and other basic necessities. Even with the oil-for-food arrangement, parts of Iraqi society suffered from hunger and lack of clean water and medicine. The United States charged that Saddam's government was using the oil money to enrich itself, not to help relieve hunger. Iraq complained that the United States

On December 16, 1998, U.S. president Bill Clinton announced a new campaign against Iraq called Operation Desert Fox.

was using the sanctions system to weaken Iraq so it could take over the country.

Perhaps encouraged by international sympathy for the hungry Iraqis, Saddam began to resist UN restrictions. For example, the Iraqi government did not fully cooperate with and even harassed the UN weapons inspectors. Unable to adequately inspect weapons sites, the United Nations pulled all its inspectors from the country in 1998. To punish Iraq for this lack of cooperation, the United States and Great Britain launched a bombing campaign called Operation Desert Fox. It had little effect. Saddam had an unshakable hold on power.

GOING
8 AFTER SADDAM

In the U.S. presidential election in 2000, the Republican candidate, George W. Bush, was declared the winner. The new president was the son of George H. W. Bush. The new President Bush chose many of his father's aides to be part of his government. These included Richard Cheney (secretary of defense for the elder Bush) as vice president and Donald Rumsfeld (an under secretary of defense under the first Bush) as secretary of defense.

A "WAR ON TERROR"

On September 11, 2001, in a coordinated attack, terrorists took control of four U.S. passenger planes. They crashed two of them into the two World Trade Center towers in New York City. The hijackers crashed another plane into the Pentagon, headquarters of the U.S. Department of Defense, near Washington, D.C. The fourth plane was probably headed for either the White House or the Capitol Building in Washington, but passengers on United Flight 93 fought the terrorists, and the plane crashed into a field in southwestern Pennsylvania. The tragedies of that day, often called "9/11," took the lives of close to 3,000 people and rocked American confidence in the security of the United States. In response, Bush declared a "War on Terror" and vowed to destroy the terrorist organization al-Qaeda (Arabic for "the base") and its leaders.

Evidence clearly connected the attacks to al-Qaeda. Its leader is a Saudi Muslim named Osama bin Laden, who had declared a jihad (holy war) against the United States and its allies.

Like many Arabs, bin Laden hated the United States for supporting Israel. But his hatred went even further. He, like many other Saudis, was furious that U.S. troops were still stationed in Saudi Arabia. They were also angry that Saudi Arabia's monarch allowed them to stay. Bin Laden supported a huge network of terrorist training camps in Afghanistan and elsewhere. Young fighters were brought to these camps and taught how to conduct terrorist attacks on airplanes, subways, power stations, shopping centers, and other targets.

ATTACKING AFGHANISTAN

Afghanistan was ruled by a group of strictly religious young men known as the Taliban (the students). The Taliban supported bin Laden's jihad and allowed al-Qaeda to maintain a large network of terrorist camps in their country. Bin Laden and his top aides were believed to be living in Afghanistan.

Bush demanded that the Taliban government turn Osama bin Laden over to the United States and destroy the al-Qaeda terrorist camps. When they refused, U.S. and British forces—with support from Pakistan, Uzbekistan, and Tajikistan—joined Afghan rebel groups in November 2001 and launched an operation to drive the Taliban from power and destroy al-Qaeda's network of support.

This required hard fighting in mountains and deserts, but there was never any doubt that the U.S. military could blast the Taliban from power. Much of the worst fighting occurred in caves in eastern Afghanistan, where members of al-Qaeda were said to be hiding. U.S. forces used massive concussion bombs, which sent shock waves throughout cave tunnels and eventually used up all the air inside.

U.S. Marines move into southern Afghanistan in late November during the start of the war against the Taliban and al-Qaeda.

The Taliban was routed, and Osama bin Laden went into hiding. By January 2002, the United States had helped put together a new government in the Afghan capital of Kabul. Real control of the rest of Afghanistan stayed in the hands of local warlords, as it had been for many centuries. U.S. soldiers and their allies stayed on in Afghanistan to protect the new government and to continue hunting for Osama bin Laden.

THE AXIS OF EVIL

On January 29, 2002, delivering the annual televised presidential speech called the State of the Union address, President Bush described Iraq, Iran, and North Korea as an "axis of evil." He said that the governments of these countries supported or sold weapons of mass destruction (WMD) to terrorist groups. These nations, he said, were dangerous and a threat to the world. Weapons of mass destruction include nuclear bombs, chemical weapons, and biological weapons.

Bush's use of the word *axis* implied that these countries were enemies, as were the Axis nations of Germany, Italy, and Japan in World War II. Some people welcomed Bush's hard-line approach to threats against the United States. They believed the United States needed to act aggressively to stop potential threats to the United States. But Bush's comment worried many Americans and observers overseas. They wondered whether the president would try to attack these countries.

The United States soon signaled that Iraq was a definite target. In February 2002, the United States went to the UN to request that weapons inspections in Iraq be resumed. President Bush said he hoped that the UN inspectors could discover whether Iraq was secretly stockpiling WMDs. Iraq refused to let the inspectors into the country.

President Bush and many of his advisers said that if Iraq still had hidden WMDs, Saddam would use these weapons against his enemies. He had already used chemical weapons against the Iranians and the Kurds, and he had threatened to use WMDs against Israel. Bush also said that he feared that Saddam might sell weapons to terrorist groups who would use them, possibly against the United States.

Saddam's refusals to cooperate with UN weapons inspectors at various times from 1991 to 2003 suggested that he was indeed hiding weapons. He had lied and hidden weapons before. Although Saddam had agreed to eliminate all of his WMDs after the war in 1991, UN inspectors found one kind of nerve gas later in the 1990s. When they first accused him of concealing the gas, Saddam claimed that Iraq had only produced 200 liters of it. In fact, he had produced thousands of liters.

Through the spring and summer of 2002, the Bush administration publicly threatened to take military action against Iraq. They pointed out that Saddam's rule was evil, brutal, corrupt, and untrustworthy. They said that removing Saddam and creating a democracy in Iraq would help the entire Middle East. The administration said that Saddam might have connections to al-Qaeda. Bush and his advisers wanted a regime change, a polite phrase for removing Saddam from power.

Weapons of Mass Destruction

The term "weapons of mass destruction," or WMDs, refers to weapons that can cause massive numbers of casualties—dead or wounded.

BIOLOGICAL WEAPONS

Anthrax is a natural bacterium that can infect the lungs, causing death. In nature it does not often infect people. Anthrax makes a convenient weapon because under dry conditions, the bacteria produce spores that can survive for a long time without food or water. If they are inhaled, these spores come to life and reproduce in warm, moist places such as the human respiratory tract.

Biological toxins are taken from biological sources and can be used to poison air and water supplies. An example of a biological toxin is botulinum toxin, a kind of nerve agent that causes paralysis. The toxin is produced by a bacterium. In 1991 Iraq possessed enough of the deadly botulinum toxin to kill everyone in the world.

One potential viral weapon that is greatly feared is smallpox. The once deadly smallpox disease was eventually wiped out. Most laboratory samples of the virus were destroyed, but some samples were kept by laboratories in the United States and the Soviet Union. Experts worry that terrorists might use a stolen virus to kill many people before they could be vaccinated.

CHEMICAL WEAPONS

Iraq was known to possess and have used several types of chemical weapons, including nerve agents such as VX gas, sarin, and tabun. Nerve agents cause paralysis and death by injuring the human nervous system. Iraq was also known to have produced and used blistering agents such as mustard gas, which cause burning and blistering on the skin or inside the body.

NUCLEAR WEAPONS

Nuclear weapons include fission bombs and fusion bombs. They use radioactive materials to cause massive explosions that can wipe out entire cities. Another kind of nuclear weapon is a dirty "bomb." A dirty bomb could spread deadly radioactive material over a large area, killing thousands or even millions of people. Iraq openly worked to develop nuclear weapons until its nuclear reactor, used to make uranium, was destroyed in a raid by Israel in 1981. The United States suspected that Iraq continued to develop nuclear weapons after that, using imported uranium.

The Bush administration's proposal to launch an attack on Iraq was based on the idea of acting preemptively—taking action to stop something before it actually happens. The administration claimed that the WMDs that Iraq was suspected of having were so dangerous that the United States had a legitimate reason to attack. Bush and

U.S. president George W. Bush addressed the United Nations on September 12, 2002. He asked UN member nations to support a U.S.-led preemptive attack on Iraq.

his pro-war advisers believed that a preemptive attack was necessary. It would prevent Iraq from using the WMDs or selling them to terrorists or to other countries. The idea that the United States had a special right to attack other countries to protect it from WMDs and terrorism in the future became known as the "Bush Doctrine."

ASKING FOR EVIDENCE

Critics of the proposal pointed out that preemptive attack is forbidden by international law. If one country is allowed to attack another based only on what might happen in the future, any country could use the same reasoning to attack any other country it wished.

They pointed out that Iraq hadn't attacked the United States or its allies since 1991. Saddam's government, although oppressive, was considered legitimate by the world community. Iraq had a seat at the United Nations. But Saddam wasn't living up to the 1991 cease-fire agreement when

he denied access to UN weapons inspectors. His actions made other UN members suspicious that he had weapons to hide.

Critics of Bush's policy asked for hard evidence that Iraq was storing WMDs and that it had connections to al-Qaeda. They said that without such evidence, a preemptive attack was unjust. The Bush administration responded that it had evidence to prove Iraq possessed WMDs but couldn't share this proof because it would weaken national security. (The evidence was later proven to have been based on faulty information.)

Worries about security after the horror of the 9/11 attacks hung over the U.S. debate about Iraq. Polls showed that a majority of Americans were willing to support the president, even without seeing evidence against Iraq, because they were worried about another terrorist attack.

The U.S. Congress gave Bush an important vote of support on October 11, 2002. The House of Representatives voted 296 to 133 in favor of a resolution authorizing the United States to take military action against Iraq, with or without the UN's approval.

UN weapons inspectors investigate a military-industrial compound in Rashidiya, Iraq, located 12 miles northeast of Baghdad.

Later that day, the Senate approved a similar resolution 77 to 23.

INSPECTORS RETURN

Under threat of war by the United States, Iraq changed its mind and allowed UN weapons inspectors to return to Iraq in November 2002. A new inspection team was put together under the leadership of Hans Blix, a Swedish scientist. Another team, looking specifically for nuclear weapons, was directed by Mohamed el-Baradei, an Egyptian, who headed the International Atomic Energy Agency.

After searching Saddam's palaces and other buildings that had been off-limits to earlier inspectors, Blix's and el-Baradei's teams found no evidence of WMD storage or manufacture in Iraq. But they also pointed out that they did not receive Saddam's full and complete cooperation. Also, the Iraqi government never accounted for tons of illegal arms that had disappeared

While the inspectors worked, the United States began another military buildup in the Gulf. The logistics (practical arrangements) were simpler than in 1990 and 1991. The United States already had more than 10,000 troops and a good deal of military hardware in Gulf nations. U.S. fighters based at Incirlik in southern Turkey had been patrolling Iraq's no-fly zones for years. In the fall of 2002, Qatar gave the United States permission to build a military base there.

A CONTROVERSIAL DECISION

Bush tried to repeat his father's success at putting together a broad coalition to fight Saddam. However, he failed to gather the same diverse support. Great Britain, led by Prime Minister Tony Blair, was the only nation to offer any large-scale contribution to the invasion force. Spain, Poland, and Australia also volunteered small numbers of troops. This time, a war against Iraq was going to be a U.S. and British operation. From December 2002 to March 2003, the

United States sought UN approval to use force against Iraq. At the same time, U.S. officials said that the United States needed to act in its own best interests no matter what the UN decided. It could no longer trust its national security to the UN. France, Germany, and Russia accused the United States of unilateralism (willingness to take action without allies).

On January 18, 2003, millions of people marched through cities in the United States and around the world protesting U.S. plans to attack Iraq. Even in Spain and Great Britain, whose governments sided with the United States, the public was overwhelmingly opposed to war. Fewer than 20 percent of all Europeans said they supported a war. In the United States, opinion polls showed that most Americans supported a new war against Iraq only if the United Nations approved one.

On February 24, 2003, the United States, Spain, and Great Britain introduced a resolution to the UN Security Council declaring that Iraq had used up its last chance to respond to questions about its WMDs. On March 7, the three nations revised their resolution, saying that Iraq had to disarm by March 17 or risk war.

Few nations in the Security Council supported the resolution. The only members of the council willing to vote in favor of it were the three sponsors (the United States, Great Britain, and Spain) and Bulgaria, far short of the nine necessary votes. France promised to veto it. On March 17, the United States, Britain, and Spain withdrew their resolution rather than face defeat.

That same day, the UN ordered its personnel, including the weapons inspectors, to leave Iraq. U.S. secretary of state Colin Powell announced that the United States had assembled a "coalition of the willing" to attack Iraq without approval by the UN. Of the 30 nations of the coalition, the United States, Britain, Poland, Australia, Denmark, and Spain were able to con-

In 2003 thousands of demonstrators across the United States and the world protested President Bush's decision to declare war on Iraq.

A Tomahawk cruise missile is fired from the USS *Milius* in the Persian Gulf on March 22, 2003. Tomahawk missiles were used in the first stage of the attacks during Operation Iraqi Freedom.

tribute troops or ships to the effort. Some of the other nations in the coalition were Albania, Italy, Latvia, Slovakia, and Uzbekistan. Not on this list were some of the most crucial partners the United States had in the earlier Iraqi war—the Arab nations of Kuwait, Bahrain, and Qatar. Although they were serving as bases for the new U.S. effort, these Arab states were reluctant to publicize their help for a war that was very unpopular in the Arab world.

OPERATION IRAQI FREEDOM

On March 18, 2003, President Bush announced that the United States and its allies would attack Iraq unless Saddam Hussein and his two sons, Uday and Qusay, left Iraq within 48 hours. They did not leave. On March 20, U.S. and British soldiers began an invasion of Iraq to oust Saddam from power. The Bush government referred to the invasion as Operation Iraqi Freedom.

The first attacks of the war came with 36 Tomahawk cruise missiles and two F-117 stealth bombers aiming for the same bunker, a strongly built underground room, in downtown Baghdad. The bombs dropped by the F-117s were "bunker-busters," able to burrow underground, penetrate the hardened walls of a bunker, and explode inside. The U.S. military explained that this concentrated attack on one bunker was an attempt to kill Saddam Hussein and other top Iraqi leaders believed to be meeting there. Saddam was not in the targeted bunker. A few days later, he appeared on a video urging Iraqis to resist the U.S. invaders.

The invasion of Iraq took about three weeks. U.S. and British troops moved in by land from Kuwait and were flown in by helicopter from ships in the Gulf. The general movement of troops was from south to north. The coalition partners had hoped to open a front in northern Iraq as well, with

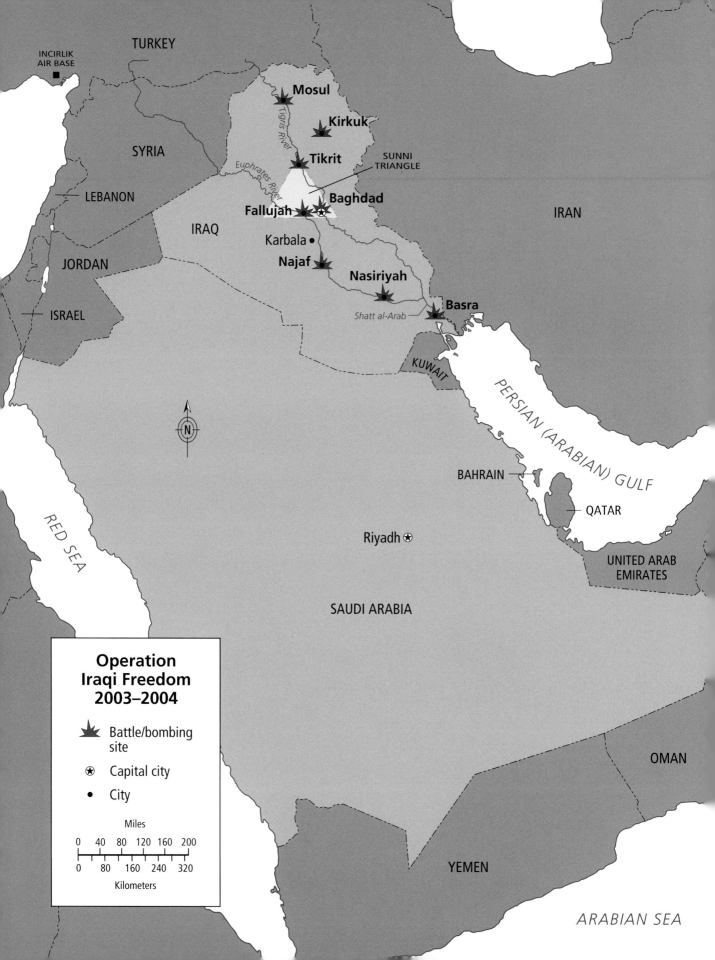

Warplanes on Autopilot

By the 2003 war, the U.S. military had developed new, high-tech planes called RQ-4A Global Hawk surveillance planes. Piloted by computers, they fly high in the sky to take pictures of potential targets and relay the pictures back to command centers.

The U.S. military also had RQ-1 Predator systems made up of teams of four aircraft to provide intelligence from three cameras and radar. Each plane (right) carries cameras in its nose. The planes don't have pilots in them. They are supported by a crew of 55 people on the ground. One of them is the pilot flying the plane by remote control. The others deal with the mechanical side and with the information the planes send back.

troops marching from Turkey into mostly Kurdish parts of northern Iraq. Turkey's parliament, however, refused permission for U.S. troops to set up bases in Turkey.

British troops took primary responsibility for the Shiite areas of southern Iraq, including the city of Basra. U.S. troops headed for the vital bridges across the Euphrates River. They wanted to secure them before Iraqi defenders could blow them up and prevent U.S. troops from quickly crossing the river. As the coalition troops moved north, they left behind supply stations that could be linked together into a solid line of support from Kuwait northward. To ensure quick progress toward Baghdad, the U.S. forward units marched right past many cities in southern Iraq rather than slowing down for street-by-street city fighting. Follow-up units fought to secure the cities later and ran into stiff resistance at Nasiriyah and Najaf.

A U.S. Marine wounded in fighting in Nasiriyah is helped to safety.

HARDWARE AND ARMAMENTS

THE UNITED STATES

In 1991 and again in 2003, the U.S.-led coalition forces used the newest in military technology—often with help from satellites in space.

By Air

- The F-117A Nighthawk and the B-2 Spirit are stealth aircraft that look more like UFOs than planes. They were designed to pass through all aircraft detection systems.
- Bombers included B-52s, which had been used as far back as the 1950s. They were adapted with modern technology to carry bombs, mines, and missiles. The B-1 is a fast, maneuverable new bomber loaded with modern electronics and guided and unguided bombs.

- Fighter planes included the F-15s *(left)*, F-16s, and later the F-22s. The F/A-18 can function as both a fighter and a bomber. Fighters were used to fly through enemy defenses and to fight against Iraqi aircraft. They carried air-to-air missiles and cannons and sometimes bombs for ground attacks. F-15 fighters can fly as fast as 1,875 miles per hour (more than two times the speed of sound).

- AV-8B Harrier aircraft can take off and land vertically. These fighter planes can be launched from helicopter pads at sea.

- Numerous helicopters, including Apache attack helicopters *(right)*, flew low and deep behind enemy lines, to attack, to do surveillance, and to rescue downed soldiers.
- E-3 Sentry AWACS, with their huge radar domes, performed surveillance, watching troop and equipment movements from high above the battlefield.
- "Smart bombs" (bombs that can be laser-guided or that would seek out targets marked with infrared light) ushered in a new era in warfare with long-distance, precise strikes.
- Radar-controlled antimissile systems intercepted Iraqi missiles with Patriot missiles. This was an essential weapon in the Persian Gulf War. One of the greatest fears was of Iraq firing long-range missiles equipped with a chemical or biological warhead.

By Sea

- World War II battleships and modern cruisers patrolled the sea. They shelled Iraqi positions in 1991 and launched cruise missiles in 2003.
- Nuclear attack submarines rose from beneath the waves to launch cruise missiles at targets in Iraq.
- Tomahawk cruise missiles *(right),* which can turn corners and strike within feet of preprogrammed targets, were launched from the sea to attack targets in Iraq.
- Six aircraft carriers—capable of carrying more than 90 aircraft each—created airstrips at sea to bring the planes closer to their targets.

By Land

- M-1A1 and M-60 tanks have special armor to protect them from attacks.
- Lighter armored vehicles such as the M2/M3 Bradley Fighting Vehicles and the LAV-25 Light Armored Vehicles can move faster and carry more troops than the tanks.
- Howitzers (giant cannons) can fire shells at targets miles away.

In Space

- Global Positioning Satellites (GPS) and communications satellites provide navigation information to planes, ships, ground units, and smart weapons.
- Surveillance satellites helped locate potential targets.

IRAQ

Saddam Hussein found himself outgunned in 1991 and in 2003, but the Iraqi military did possess some advanced weapons. Saddam had bought weapons and technology from the Soviet Union, western Europe, and even the United States. In some cases, Iraqis modified these weapons to make them even deadlier.

Aircraft Iraq had a number of French Mirage F-1 and Soviet MiG fighter jets as well as French and Soviet helicopters. During the air war, these aircraft were used to defend against coalition aircraft. After the third day of Desert Storm, though, many of the Iraqi fighters used their planes to escape to Iran, either for their own safety or to save the planes.

Ground Units Iraq was also well supplied with tanks and armored units. In addition, they used highly accurate G-5 howitzer cannons, surface-to-surface rocket systems, and surface-to-air missiles (SAM) against coalition aircraft.

Al-Hussein missiles were Soviet Scud missiles that had been improved by the Iraqis to double their range. In Desert Storm, this allowed them to be launched at targets as far away as Israel. The modified missile launchers could also be moved quickly, which prevented the United States from finding and destroying them right away.

The Fedayeen Saddam

During the 2003 invasion and occupation of Iraq, U.S. soldiers often faced guerrilla forces disguised as civilians and devoted to Saddam's regime. One of these groups of specially trained guerrillas was the Fedayeen Saddam.

The Fedayeen was a paramilitary group (a group outside of the regular military) containing tens of thousands of young men. Before the United States invaded Iraq, Saddam had used the Fedayeen to execute civilians as a way to control opposition. The Fedayeen was organized and directed by Saddam's son Uday.

Coalition troops capture two guerrilla fighters (blindfolded) from the Fedayeen Saddam after a raid on a house in Baghdad in April 2003.

As U.S. forces advanced toward Baghdad, resistance from the Fedayeen and from some regular units of Iraq's army was light, and the troops made rapid progress. No major battles stopped the advance toward the city. U.S. forces captured Baghdad's Saddam International Airport on April 3. Republican Guard

U.S. troops take aim against possible resistance fighters as the coalition closes in on Saddam International Airport in Baghdad on April 3, 2003.

Kurdish fighters celebrate after they secured the city of Kirkuk on April 10, 2003.

units fought for about 24 hours to hold off the Americans, but without success. From the airport, renamed Baghdad International, U.S. troops pushed northward toward the city. Resistance was light, and U.S. troops captured the city of Baghdad on April 9.

Saddam and his forces were nowhere to be seen in Baghdad. It was thought that he had retreated to his hometown of Tikrit to make a last stand. Certain that Saddam had left Baghdad, many Iraqis came out into the streets to show their contempt for their former ruler.

Kurdish troops captured the northern city of Kirkuk the next day. On April 13, Tikrit, fell to U.S. soldiers. All of Iraq was under U.S. and British control. But Saddam, his sons, and many top Iraqi leaders were nowhere to be found.

OCCUPYING
IRAQ

On May 1, 2003, Bush declared, "Major combat operations in Iraq have ended. In the battle of Iraq, the United States and our allies have prevailed." Bush was right in that no Iraqi government or army existed anymore to challenge coalition troops. Combat, however, was far from over.

A NEED FOR POLICE

The situation in Iraq was chaotic. In Basra, in Baghdad, and elsewhere, looting (stealing from stores and public buildings in a time of crisis) occurred as soon as the public realized that Saddam's forces were gone. Coalition troops generally stood aside and did not try to stop the looting. They were not trained in police methods for controlling crowds of civilians. Iraq's city police forces still existed, but they were disorganized and too small to control the large number of looters. The coalition had not sent police to follow up the invasion force, possibly because U.S. war planners expected a generally peaceful aftermath to the invasion.

There were a few celebrations at the beginning. Most Iraqis were very happy to see an end to Saddam's rule. But many Iraqis became disillusioned with the coalition as the Americans settled into Baghdad. Under U.S. military rule, Iraqis continued to live without electricity, drinking water, safe roads, and other necessities of life.

They worried that the coalition would not be able to control rivalries among Iraq's many religious and ethnic groups.

About 400 political parties sprang up in Iraq after Saddam was deposed. Some politically ambitious leaders on all sides—including Kurds, several Shiite clerics, some Sunnis who feared a Shiite takeover, and Iraqis who had recently returned from exile in the United States—founded militia groups of private, part-time soldiers. It was part of the parties' strategy to build up their own forces so they could compete for power whenever a new Iraqi government was formed. The militia often provided order in areas where there were no police or military to do it. Some of these armed groups and some Iraqis in general believed it was time for the Americans and their partners to leave. Various groups formed to obstruct the coalition occupation. These anti-coalition fighters hoped to make the occupation so deadly and expensive that the coalition troops would be forced to leave.

HITTING THE INFRASTRUCTURE

Just before coalition troops captured Baghdad, the city's electric power was cut off. The blackout was probably part of an early anti-coalition tactic. Their plan was to sabotage Iraq's infrastructure, the basic systems (such as electricity or water supply) on which everyday life depends. The resistance also targeted oil facilities, especially pipelines.

The invasion force had been careful to avoid damaging these systems. The coalition would have to reconstruct (rebuild) Iraq after the invasion, and a working infrastructure would make that easier. The U.S.-led force hoped especially to keep Iraq's oil industry working. Oil money could help pay for the reconstruction. Most important, the Americans were eager to show that life would be better without Saddam. That would be hard to do if Iraqis had no electricity, drinking water, telephone service, or passable roads.

CHECKPOINTS

To search for saboteurs (those deliberately damaging the infrastructure), wanted Baathists, and weapons, coalition forces set up checkpoints along major roads. The anti-occupation insurgents, those fighting against the U.S.-led government, sent suicide bombers to these checkpoints. When the bomber was stopped, he or she would blow up the car, themselves, and any coalition soldiers who were nearby.

Soldiers at the checkpoints became suspicious of nearly everyone. In some cases, jittery soldiers shot at Iraqis who seemed to be behaving suspiciously, and some innocent Iraqis were killed. The insurgents used these incidents to condemn the occupation forces.

HUNTING FOR SADDAM

As the Iraqi insurgent groups grew stronger, the Bush administration said that the trouble came from a few frustrated Saddam loyalists. If the United States could catch Saddam and his cronies, the attacks would stop. The effort to find Saddam and other top Baathist leaders was a top priority.

Many of the top Baath Party officials surrendered soon after the invasion. On April 25, Tariq Aziz, Iraq's former foreign minister turned himself in. Others were captured or

Most Wanted Playing Cards

Capturing the leaders of the Baath Party had been a coalition goal from the start. One day before U.S. troops took Baghdad, the U.S. Department of Defense issued a deck of 55 playing cards—one blank card, two jokers (with explanations of Arabic military terms), and 52 cards with the names of Iraqis whom the United States wanted most to capture. Saddam Hussein was the ace of spades. His sons Qusay and Uday were the aces of clubs and hearts.

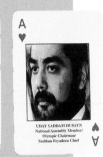

Qusay (left), Saddam (center), and Uday (right) are featured on these "Most Wanted" playing cards.

killed. Still others, including Saddam and his two sons, avoided capture for months.

On July 22, 2003, a special U.S. task force hunting for former Baath Party leaders raided a house in the northern city of Mosul. The house's owner claimed Saddam's sons, Uday and Qusay, were inside. After a fierce gun battle, U.S. forces emerged with the bodies of both men. To prove that the dead men really were Uday and Qusay, the U.S. military displayed the bodies for television cameras.

The search for Saddam himself went on. Then on December 13, 2003, special operations troops raided a farm south of Tikrit and found Saddam hiding in a small covered hole in the farmyard—referred to by the military as a "spider hole." (The term "spider hole" comes from the way trap-door spiders catch their prey. The spider builds a burrow in the ground lined with spiderweb and covers the hole with a trapdoor made of soil and spiderweb. The spider hides in the burrow and jumps out when prey approaches.) Saddam, looking

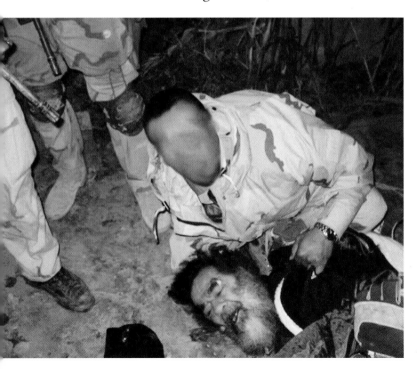

A captured Saddam Hussein is pulled from his hiding place on December 13, 2003. The face of the soldier extracting Saddam is blurred to protect his identity against retaliation by Saddam's faithful followers.

dirty and wearing a long beard, surrendered without a fight. U.S. troops jailed Saddam under very tight security, and diplomats began working out the details of his eventual trial for war crimes.

GOVERNING IRAQ

The first U.S. official to govern Iraq was General Jay Garner, who functioned as a military governor. As chaos in Iraq grew, many problems were blamed on Garner, and he was removed from his position. L. Paul Bremer took over as civilian administrator of Iraq in May 2003.

Bremer led a body known as the Coalition Provisional Authority (CPA), which was made up of representatives of the nations in the coalition. In August 2003, the CPA appointed a group of Iraqis, known as the Iraqi Governing Council (IGC) to help revive Iraqi self-rule and write a new constitution, a plan for government, for Iraq. The short-term goal was for the CPA to hand over authority to Iraqis on July 1, 2004, while coalition troops stayed in Iraq to provide protection.

Iraqi Governing Council

The IGC was originally made up of 25 members from Iraq's various ethnic and religious groups. Three of the original members were women. One of the women, Aqila al-Hashimi, was shot to death in September 2003. Another one of the original 25, Ezzedine Salim, was killed by a car bomb in May 2004.

The IGC also included Ahmed Chalabi, Saddam's opponent who had lived for a long time in the United States. Chalabi had won the confidence of some members of the Bush administration long before the invasion of Iraq. The U.S. government paid Chalabi's organization, the Iraqi National Congress, to provide information about Iraq, and many people expected the United States to name him Iraq's new leader.

It was later learned that information Chalabi had given to the CIA before the war about conditions in Iraq was false. The United States no longer supports him, and the new Iraqi government wants to arrest him for earlier crimes.

THE IRAQI POINT OF VIEW

By 2003 Iraqis had lived through more than a decade of trade sanctions, which kept them from buying needed supplies from other countries. They had also faced periodic air raids by U.S. and British planes. Over time, Iraqi opinion had turned against these countries. Even some Iraqis who hated Saddam came to view Americans in the 2003 war not as liberators but as oppressors. Every accidental civilian casualty seemed to some to confirm the idea that the United States was a brutal occupying force. "The enemy of my enemy is my friend," runs an old Arab saying. But faced with heavy civilian casualties during and after the war, even some Iraqis who opposed Saddam Hussein came to see the United States as another enemy.

The long-term plan is to hold an election and make Iraq's governance truly democratic.

IRAQI SECURITY FORCES

When Bremer took over leadership of the CPA in May 2003, the CPA faced serious security problems in Iraq. By the summer of 2003, the insurgents were killing an average of one and a half Americans each day and even more Iraqi civilians. In August 2003, a cement truck loaded with explosives destroyed the Baghdad headquarters of the United Nations, killing many diplomats and causing the UN to leave Iraq because it was too dangerous.

In an attempt to put an end to such attacks, the CPA established and began training several forces made up of Iraqis. These forces would be the beginnings of the move to train Iraqi groups to protect their own citizens. It was one step toward transferring power and control to the Iraqi people. One of these groups, the Civil Defense Force (CDF), was meant to fight alongside coalition troops and patrol cities where the insurgents were strong. Another, the new Iraqi army, was supposed to patrol Iraq's borders and help repel any foreign attack on Iraqi territory. The CPA also established the Iraqi Facilities Protection Force to guard oil installations, water supplies, and other infrastructure elements. There was also a new Iraqi customs office and a new police force.

Most of the people hired for these forces were former members of the regular Iraqi army who had not shown any special loyalty to Saddam. Neither did they have any special loyalty to the coalition. They

The UN headquarters in eastern Baghdad smolders after it was bombed by Iraqi insurgents in August 2003.

U.S. soldiers oversee the training of new Iraqi police cadets in August 2003. Iraqis took jobs with the Coalition Provisional Authority to avoid unemployment, but some of the soldiers abandoned their jobs to join insurgent forces.

joined the forces mostly to have a job. Unemployment in Iraq was high, and the CPA paid its soldiers very well.

Insurgents targeted CPA-paid soldiers, especially the Civil Defense Force, to punish them for helping the coalition. Ordinary Iraqis looked forward to the security the newly trained groups would bring. For the most part, Iraqis are angry with the insurgents, who are trying to break down any order the country has gained.

Most of the security forces did their job and obeyed orders, but a few turned against the coalition. This was particularly true when, in April 2004, heavy fighting took place in Fallujah and cities near it. Some estimates are that about 12 percent of the CDF who meant to help the coalition forces pacify Fallujah turned against

their units and joined the anti-coalition fighting.

LOOKING FOR HELP

When President Bush launched the invasion of Iraq, he was confident that the United States and its few coalition partners could succeed without the support of the United Nations or many traditional U.S. allies. But this approach was very expensive. The U.S. Congressional Budget Office estimated that occupying Iraq would cost the United States about $29 billion every year. In August 2003, Bush addressed the United Nations General Assembly asking for support in Iraq, but UN members were not anxious to become involved in a war they had not approved.

In October 2003, the U.S. Congress voted to set aside $87 billion for the reconstruction

Uncovering Mass Graves

The international organization Human Rights Watch says that about 300,000 Iraqis "went missing" during Saddam Hussein's rule. Most were killed by the Iraqi army or secret police. Many ended up in unmarked mass graves in various parts of the country.

Following the collapse of Saddam's regime, Iraqis began to search for and uncover these mass graves. The first such grave was discovered in the town Imam Bakr in central Iraq—it contained the remains of between forty and fifty people who were involved in the 1991 Shiite uprising against Saddam. By 2004 more than one hundred other graves had been unearthed, containing more than 100,000 victims.

of Iraq and Afghanistan. Huge as this amount was, it will not be enough. Bush still hoped other nations and the United Nations might contribute.

Bush got promises of some help at a conference of potential donors in October 2003, including about $27 million from Germany and about $233 million from the European Union, which included a contribution from France. It was clear that the financial burden of occupying and rebuilding Iraq was largely on U.S. shoulders.

THE SUNNI TRIANGLE

Fallujah was one of several cities north and west of Baghdad in an area known as the Sunni Triangle. The Sunni population of this area resisted the U.S. occupation more fiercely than most other Iraqis. Some of them remained loyal to the Baath Party, which had favored Sunnis during its reign. Others were worried that if the coalition's plan for elections in Iraq went forward, the Shiites would take over and the Sunnis would face discrimination.

Sunni insurgents repeatedly attacked coalition patrols in the Sunni Triangle. They set off car bombs when troop transport vehicles passed. Coalition civilians, who had come to work on the reconstruction of Iraq, were attacked or kidnapped in Sunni Triangle cities. Four U.S. civilians were murdered in the spring of 2004, and their bodies

The face of a captured U.S. civilian hostage is broadcast on Arabic-language television on May 6, 2004. Kidnappings were on the rise in 2004, as Iraqi insurgents found new ways to hamper coalition occupation and rebuilding efforts in Iraq.

A blast in a train station in Madrid, Spain, blew a hole in this train on March 11, 2004. Islamic terrorists targeted countries, including Spain, that had contributed to the U.S. war and occupation of Iraq.

were burned, then hung from a bridge. U.S. troops responded by firing on anti-coalition fighter positions, then setting up a two-week siege. Relative calm returned after the marines enlisted a former Iraqi army officer, Mohammed Latif, to make peace in the city.

Although the Shiite areas of Iraq were fairly peaceful in the early days of the occupation, cities such as Najaf and Karbala soon became centers of resistance. Moqtada al-Sadr, a young religious leader in Najaf, preached to Shiites to rise up against the foreign occupiers. Al-Sadr had a large militia and called repeatedly on his followers to kill Americans. Clashes with his followers in Shiite areas increased in spring 2004. U.S. forces hoped to arrest al-Sadr on suspicion of murdering another Shiite cleric in 2003. But they were held back for fear of violating holy places in Najaf. Al-Sadr took full advantage of these sanctuaries. He stayed in the mosques and stored military equipment in them.

The combined insurgency of Sunni and Shiite areas made April and May of 2004 very deadly months for U.S. troops. In April 2004, an average of five U.S. soldiers were killed a day and remained at about three per day in May.

FOREIGN FIGHTERS

As Iraqis of both Sunni and Shiite communities stepped up their anti-coalition activity, foreign fighters joined the struggle. Militants from Saudi Arabia, Iran, Syria, and other countries crossed into Iraq to join the jihad against the United States. They also hit other coalition nations on their home ground.

In March 2004, coordinated explosions at three train stations in Madrid, Spain, killed about 200 people and wounded about 2,000 others. Spanish authorities suspected Jordanian terrorists of planting the bombs to punish Spain for participating in the coalition. Days later, Spain's election turned out of office the government that supported the United States and the new prime minister promised to take Spanish troops out of Iraq.

MEDICAL CARE

Medical personnel in Desert Storm faced problems that were different from those of earlier wars. First, the United States had to be prepared for the fact that Iraq might use WMDs. Iraq had used chemical warfare against Iran and against its own citizens, and it was expected to use them again against coalition soldiers. Iraq was also suspected of having biological and possibly nuclear weapons.

Soldiers were vaccinated against known biological weapon agents such as anthrax and were provided with protective equipment and antidotes to poison gases. Field hospitals and other medical facilities had to be prepared to treat the effects of these weapons too. By the time U.S. forces entered Iraq again in 2003, they had mobile shelters that looked like inflated tents. These shelters protected medical teams and patients from the possibility of being contaminated by chemicals, bacteria, or viruses, as well as from the heat and dust outside.

No chemical, biological, or nuclear weapons seem to have been used during either war. Instead, medical teams had to deal with casualties due to wounds from gunfire, explosions, and accidents, as well as medical complaints linked to the desert environment.

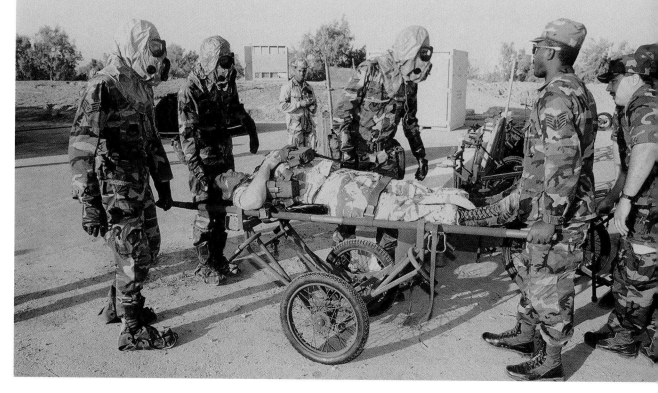

U.S. medical personnel, some wearing nuclear-biological-chemical warfare gear, transport a patient on a litter while taking part in a mass casualty exercise during Operation Desert Shield.

One of the most common medical problems that doctors saw among soldiers in 2003 was pneumonia. Soldiers breathed in tiny bits of desert sand floating in the air. The particles weakened their lungs, and pneumonia bacteria set in. Fortunately, pneumonia is fairly easy to treat.

U.S. casualties in both wars were treated on the spot and at medical facilities. Helicopter ambulances followed the front lines as soldiers advanced. In less than two hours after a battle began, as many as six patients could be loaded onto the helicopters. On them, three medics (military people trained in first aid) provided basic treatment as the wounded were flown back to fully equipped surgical teams in hospitals on a ship or in Kuwait or Saudi Arabia.

With years of experience in the Gulf region, military planners and medical specialists made constant progress in improving the speed with which injuries could be attended to. In addition to helicopter ambulances, combat medics, and surgical teams, military medical care included mobile army hospitals. For example, the U.S. Army's 86th Combat Support Hospital was able to move an entire forty-four-bed section of a hospital in 1991 from Kuwait into Iraq, following U.S. forces. It could be set up in two hours to begin tending to casualties as soon as they occurred.

In an article in *The Mercury* (June 2003), the magazine of the military medical forces, one medic tells of his experiences during the 2003 war with Iraq:

> We can't perform miracles out there, but we can stabilize people until the patient can get back to the proper medical . . . facilities. . . . Many times I've heard bullets flying close over my head. Of course you're scared out there, but you know that there are soldiers counting on you to be there when called. [Combat medics] need to remain focused and treat the casualty.
>
> —Medical specialist Carl Smith,
> 2nd Battalion, 325th Airborne Infantry Regiment

Jobless Iraqi men stand in line at the unemployment office in Samawa, Iraq, in January 2004 in hopes of finding employment.

GETTING BACK TO SQUARE ONE

The reconstruction of Iraq was not moving as quickly as the war planners had hoped. One year after the invasion, some parts of the Iraqi economy had bounced back to pre-invasion levels. Oil production, which had fallen to almost zero, was at about pre-war levels by spring 2004. Similarly, Iraq's hospitals were about 90 percent as well supplied as they had been under Saddam.

Ever since the invasion, Iraq has suffered from high unemployment. Many men in the huge army and members of Saddam's government became unemployed after the war. More than 50 percent of Iraq's workers were without jobs for most of the first year after the invasion. By May 2004, unemployment had dropped to about 45 percent, meaning that only slightly more than half of the Iraqi workforce actually had jobs. As men are being retrained for security forces and as other parts of the economy (such as the oil industry) return to normal, these numbers should grow more quickly.

AMERICAN ATTITUDES

Immediately after the invasion of Iraq, a major poll found that about three-quarters of all Americans approved of President Bush's actions in Iraq. By May 2004, the same polling organization found that only 42 percent approved and 55 percent disapproved. U.S. troop casualties had risen, life for Iraqis in many ways hadn't much improved, and anti-coalition fighters were creating new turmoil. Progress toward an effective post-Saddam government made up entirely of Iraqis was going slowly. At this point, it wasn't clear how such a government could take control of the country so that coalition forces could leave.

The insurgent attacks on U.S. soldiers reached about 40 attacks a day in April 2004. Between May 1, 2003—when President Bush announced an end to major combat—and May 19, 2004, 466 U.S. soldiers had died in combat in Iraq. This far exceeded the number who died in the initial invasion.

The American public was also shocked in April 2004, when CBS News showed pictures of U.S. military police humiliating Iraqi prisoners at Abu Ghraib, a prison in Baghdad. Several of these photographs showed U.S. prison guards forcing naked Iraqis into embarrassing poses. The U.S. government was quick to express disgust, but the damage to the United States' international image was impossible to erase.

Critics charged that President Bush's stated reasons for going to war—Iraq's supposed weapons of mass destruction and Saddam's presumed connections to al-Qaeda—were incorrect. A year after the occupation began, the coalition had still failed to find any of the large-scale weapons programs cited by Bush as a reason to go to war. So far, no clear evidence of any Saddam connection to al-Qaeda has been discovered.

The U.S. government holds that eventually Iraq will better off because of Saddam's ouster. Troops not actively involved in the fighting have been working to improve life for the Iraqi people. In the village of Kharma, marines have built a new youth center, and elsewhere in the province, a new health clinic has been set up. The Haditha Dam is working at full power again for the first time since 1990.

Democratic senator Joseph Biden holds up one of the photos taken of Iraqi prisoners at Abu Ghraib during Senate hearings in 2004 to investigate the crimes committed by U.S. military police against Iraqi prisoners of war.

THE HOME FRONT

At first, support for President George W. Bush and the 2003 conflict in Iraq was similar to the support expressed for the Persian Gulf War. After the United States sent forces to the Gulf in March 2003, about 80 percent of Americans approved of the action, and nearly as many approved of the president himself. Then in September 2003, the UN refused to aid the United States in occupying and rebuilding Iraq. As costs rose and more U.S. service people were killed, President George W. Bush's popularity ratings dropped. They were lower than they had been before the September 11 terrorist attacks in 2001. The ratings continued to move up and down as events changed on the ground.

No WMDs were found in Iraq, and some of the original evidence for weapons of mass destruction in Iraq was found to be questionable. Some Americans who supported the war realized that the occupation of Iraq would be long, costly, and dangerous and wondered if U.S. tax dollars should be spent in this manner. The United States was going through difficult financial times, with many people out of work. However, regardless of whether they had supported or opposed the war, most of the people of the United States agreed that Saddam Hussein in prison was better than Saddam Hussein in power. And although the cost in lives has risen, most Americans support staying in Iraq for years, if necessary, until that nation's government is stable.

Protesters in Minneapolis, Minnesota, participate in a 2003 demonstration against the war in Iraq.

An army chaplain hands out clothing, shoes, food, and toys in Vedgha, Iraq, as part of the U.S. military's efforts to improve life in the villages near which they are stationed.

Elsewhere, projects from new schools to water treatment plants are under way or completed. Polls of Iraqis show mixed feelings about their situation. Still, about 70 percent of Iraqis say that they would feel less safe if coalition troops left Iraq.

Americans wonder how to get out of Iraq without leaving room for a terrible civil war among Shiites, Sunnis, Kurds, Christians, and other groups. Even some Americans who opposed the war believe that the United States has no choice but to stay until the new government is fully established and in control of security.

This will probably take several years. A war that had started out as a regional Gulf conflict has become a long-term commitment for the United States.

EPILOGUE

In early 2004, the process for handing political power back to Iraqis was under way. U.S., CPA, and IGC officials set July 1, 2004, as the deadline for the transfer of power from the IGC and CPA to an interim (temporary) Iraqi government, which would rule the country until elections could be held in January 2005. Coalition troops were scheduled to leave Iraq at the end of 2005, unless the new Iraqi government requested otherwise. The UN appointed an Algerian-born diplomat, Lakhdar Brahimi, to assess the situation. He was asked to make recommendations for who should be appointed to positions of power in the new interim Iraqi government.

Brahimi's task was difficult. Few of the candidates for high-ranking positions enjoyed much or any popular support among the Iraqi public. Throughout his time in power, Saddam Hussein had thoroughly eliminated his potential rivals, so no one living in Iraq had been able to build a popular base of support. Many of the people most qualified for high government posts were former exiles, who had worked against Saddam from foreign countries. The Iraqi public generally viewed these returning exiles with suspicion.

Nevertheless, Brahimi presented his list in late May 2004. For the top eight government posts (president, two vice presidents, prime minister, defense minister,

foreign minister, finance minister, and oil minister), he selected a mix of Shiites, Sunnis, and Kurds.

Brahimi and the United States tapped Iyad Allawi, a Shiite who had lived in exile for thirty years, to serve as prime minister, the most powerful government post. Ghazi al-Yawar, a Sunni exile, was selected as president. Several other members of the new government had already served as members of the IGC.

On June 8, 2004, the UN Security Council voted to recognize the interim leadership as Iraq's true government. With this show of support, Iraqis will be able to look to the UN—not just the United States and its coalition allies—for support in the rebuilding of the country. Shortly after the Security Council's vote, several countries offered their services to help train Iraqi police and security officials.

Brahimi also called for the creation of a national council that would have some say in government policy. The council would consist of 100 Iraqis, chosen from a group of 1,000 informally selected delegates from across the country at a convention planned for late summer 2004. The council will have the power to overturn interim government decisions with a 60 percent vote and will also have some control over the country's budget.

Critics have complained that the new administration was not popularly elected and may be little more than American "puppets." Supporters of the interim government plan insist that elections were simply not possible at this time, given the violence and lack of security in the country, but that the new interim government was the strongest possible solution to the situation.

Even before the official handover, Allawi and al-Yawar sought to increase their public standing by touring the country and appearing on television to discuss their plans with the Iraqi people. "Allawi is on all the Arab media every day talking about security," said one U.S. official. "He's visiting sites, and there are constantly images of the prime minister tackling security, which is what Iraqis care most about right now." These efforts bore fruit in the form of popular support. An independent poll of 1,000 Iraqi citizens conducted in late June found that 73 percent of Iraqis approved of Allawi as head of the new government, with 85 percent approving Ghazi al-Yawar as the new president.

On June 28, 2004, two days ahead of schedule, CPA ambassador Paul Bremer handed the reins of government to Allawi and al-Yawar in a brief secret ceremony. The early date was chosen to head off the possibility of massive terrorist attacks aimed at disrupting the June 30 handover. "I will leave Iraq confident in its future and confident in the ability of the government to meet the challenges of the future," said Bremer.

An editorial in the Iraqi newspaper *Al-Bayan* celebrated the handover. It read, "It is the ambition of every honest Iraqi to see independence, freedom, equity and justice prevalent, to enjoy the merits of peace, security and stability in this long-suffering country, whose vast human and natural potential we aspire to mobilize in a gigantic venture to build a model country."

But in the short term, the handover did little to change the day-to-day situation in Iraq. More than 130,000 foreign troops remain in the country. Insurgent attacks and kidnappings of foreign nationals continue. Allawi has shown both toughness and flexibility in his approach to the anti-occupation forces, offering amnesty (freedom from prosecution) and participation in the new Iraq to surrendering insurgents who have not killed anyone. He vowed to crush all others. "I swear to God, we will bring down the houses over your heads and fight you from room to room," he said in an interview with a Kuwaiti news agency. "But if you want to be part of the political process in Iraq, you are most welcome. Iraq is for all Iraqis."

The U.S.-led coalition has kept up its efforts to rebuild and pacify Iraq so it can eventually leave the country. A key element will be whether local government and military structures can stand on their own. If elections take place as scheduled, it still is not clear how the Kurds and the Sunnis will react to an almost certain Shiite majority in government.

In the United States, the general public remains divided about the wisdom, timing, legality, and execution of Operation Iraqi Freedom. While most Americans see the removal of Saddam Hussein as a positive development, many citizens are outraged that the Bush administration's claims about Iraq's WMD and nuclear programs have proved to be wrong. To many of these people, the war and occupation has been viewed as a terrible mistake and a horrible waste of American lives.

Those who continue to support the Bush administration's actions have noted that the burden of proof rested on Saddam. According to the agreement at the end of the 1991 war, he was required to show to the world that he had rid his country of WMDs and was no longer pursuing nuclear weapons. Many of these people believe that in a post-September 11 world, the United States needs to deal with potential terrorist threats before they can harm the United States.

A number of possible futures await Iraq. While there is a chance that Iraq could become a stable democracy, it could also be partitioned (broken up) into Kurdish, Sunni, and Shiite ministates. Tensions between these groups could erupt into civil war. A new dictatorial government might take power under another strongman. Coalition troops may need to remain in the country for many years.

Meanwhile, most Iraqi citizens are glad that Saddam's rule is in the past. A poll of Iraqi citizens taken in July 2004 show that many have optimism about the future—80 percent said they believed their lives would improve under the new government. But for the near present, Iraq remains a deeply troubled country with an uncertain future.

EVENTS OF OPERATION DESERT STORM

Invasion of Kuwait by Iraq	**August 2, 1990**
Beginning of Operation Desert Storm air war	**January 17, 1991**
Burning of Kuwaiti oil fields	**January 22–February 23, 1991**
Iraqi occupation of Khafji, Saudi Arabia	**January 29, 1991**
Ground assault on Iraqi forces in Kuwait and Iraq	**February 24, 1991**
Missile attack over al-Khobar, Saudi Arabia	**February 25, 1991**
Cease-fire	**February 28, 1991**
Battle at the Hammar Causeway in the Hammar Marshes	**March 2, 1991**
Kurdish and Shiite uprisings	**March 1991**
Missile attack on Baghdad	**June 1993**

EVENTS OF OPERATION IRAQI FREEDOM

Beginning of Operation Iraqi Freedom	**March 20, 2003**
Capture of Basra	**March 2003**
Capture of Saddam International Airport, Baghdad	**April 3, 2003**
Capture of Baghdad	**April 9, 2003**
Capture of Kirkuk	**April 10, 2003**
Capture of Tikrit	**April 13, 2003**
Uday and Qusay killed	**July 22, 2003**
Saddam Hussein captured	**December 13, 2003**
Battle with Sunni guerrillas in Fallujah	**April 2004**
Transfer of power to interim Iraqi government	**June 2004**
Battle against militia of Moqtada al-Sadr in Najaf	**August 2004**

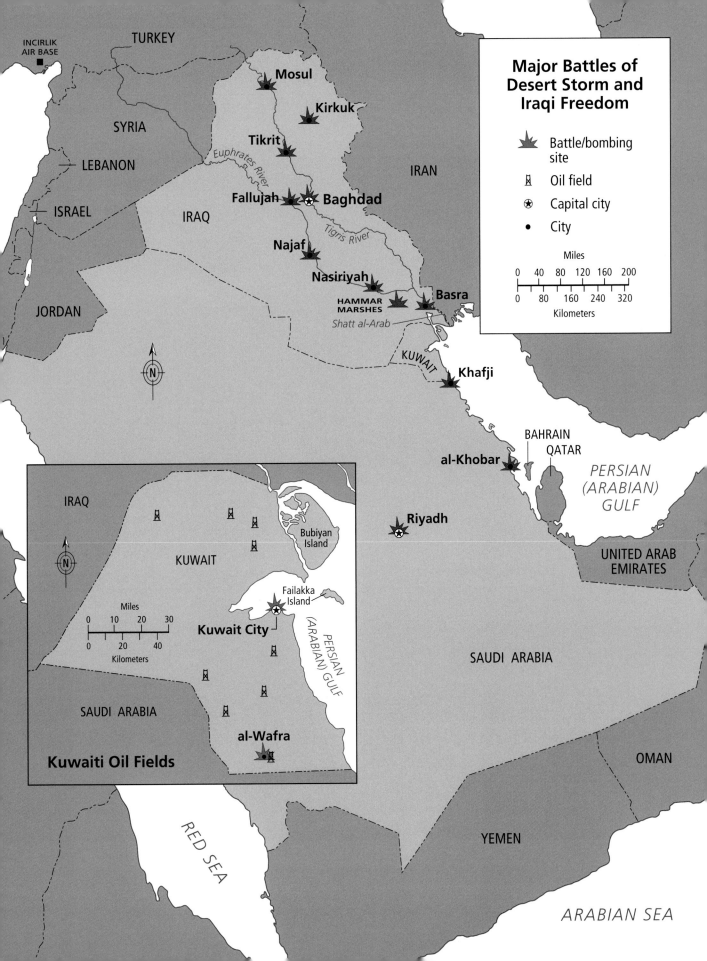

INCIRLIK AIR BASE

TURKEY

Mosul

Kirkuk

SYRIA

Tikrit

LEBANON

Euphrates River

ISRAEL

IRAN

Fallujah
Baghdad

IRAQ

Tigris River

JORDAN

Najaf

Nasiriyah

HAMMAR MARSHES

Basra

Shatt al-Arab

KUWAIT

Khafji

Major Battles of Desert Storm and Iraqi Freedom

✦ Battle/bombing site

⛏ Oil field

✪ Capital city

• City

Miles
0   40   80   120   160   200

0   80   160   240   320
Kilometers

BAHRAIN
QATAR

al-Khobar

PERSIAN (ARABIAN) GULF

Riyadh

UNITED ARAB EMIRATES

SAUDI ARABIA

IRAQ

KUWAIT

Bubiyan Island

Failakka Island

Kuwait City

PERSIAN (ARABIAN) GULF

Miles
0   10   20   30

0   20   40
Kilometers

SAUDI ARABIA

al-Wafra

Kuwaiti Oil Fields

OMAN

RED SEA

YEMEN

ARABIAN SEA

TIMELINE OF OPERATIONS DESERT STORM AND IRAQI FREEDOM

1990   Iraq invades Kuwait, August 2.
Iraq annexes Kuwait, August 8.
King Fahd decides to allow U.S. troops into Saudi Arabia, August 8.

1991   The U.S. Congress approves sending troops to Kuwait, January 12.
Desert Storm begins, January 17.
Iraq fires missiles at Israel, Saudi Arabia, and Bahrain, January 17–February 24.
Iraqi troops begin destroying Kuwaiti oil fields, January 22.
Coalition ground forces enter Kuwait and southwestern Iraq, February 24.
Scud missiles kill 28 U.S. soldiers in a barracks in al-Khobar, February 25.
Coalition soldiers take Kuwait City, February 25–26.
President George H. W. Bush orders a cease-fire, February 28.
Battle occurs between U.S. Army forces and retreating Iraqis near the
   Hammar Causeway in the Hammar Marshes, March 2.
U.S. and Iraqi leaders agree on the terms of the peace.
A no-fly zone is established in northern Iraq.
U.S. forces begin to withdraw from Iraq, March 3.
Northern Kurds and southern Shiites rebel against Saddam in March.

1993   A no-fly zone is established in southern Iraq.
Assassination attempt is made on George H. W. Bush in Kuwait in April.
The United States fires missiles at Baghdad in retaliation.

1998   Iraq bans UN weapons inspectors.

2002   George W. Bush demands the readmission of weapons inspectors. Iraq refuses
   in February.
The U.S. Congress approves military action in Iraq, October 11.
Inspectors are readmitted to Iraq in November but find no WMDs.

2003   Operation Iraqi Freedom begins as U.S. and British soldiers invade Iraq, March 20.
Saddam International Airport in Baghdad is captured, April 3.
Baghdad falls to U.S. forces, April 9.
Kurdish troops capture Kirkuk, April 10.
U.S. troops take Tikrit, April 13.
President Bush declares the end of major combat operations in Iraq, May 1.
Attacks continue on U.S. forces occupying Iraq, May–December.
Saddam Hussein is captured on December 13.

2004   Terrorist-set explosions at four train stations in Madrid kill 200 people, March 11.
Spanish government leaves coalition.
U.S. Marines fight Sunni guerrillas in Fallujah in April.
Photos of U.S. soldiers humiliating Iraqi prisoners at Abu Ghaib prison
   appear on television in April.
UN-appointed diplomat appoints new Iraqi government leaders in May.
The United States hands over control to new Iraqi government on June 28.
The militia of Mogtada al-Sadr, rebel Shiite leader, battles U.S. troops in Najaf
   in August.

GLOSSARY

Baathist: a member of the Baath Party, especially the Baath Party of Iraq. In the 1950s, the Baath Party sought to unite Arabs of various countries, but the Iraqi branch later broke away and became the ruling party of Iraq, controlled by Saddam Hussein.

coalition: a group of different people or organizations, such as governments or militaries, that work together to fulfill a common goal

Cold War: a period of hostility between the United States and the Soviet Union from the end of World War II until the collapse of the Soviet Union in 1991

conventional weapon: a weapon, such as a gun or a knife, that generally kills as it is being used. It can be an explosive that is not nuclear and leaves behind no radioactivity.

dictator: an absolute ruler who governs by the force of a military and other repressive measures, such as censorship and curtailing human rights

friendly fire: a term used since the Vietnam War (1954–1975) for weapons accidentally fired at members of one's own side

human shields: people, generally civilians or prisoners, placed in buildings and near target areas to prevent the enemy from attacking

Muslim: a believer in Islam. A Muslim follows the teachings of Muhammad, a prophet of God (Allah).

no-fly zone: an area in northern Iraq established by the UN and an area in southern Iraq established by the United States and Britain, where Iraqi planes were prohibited to fly following the 1991 Persian Gulf War

occupation: the period after a war, during which a victorious foreign army is in command of the country it has defeated

prisoner of war (POW): a soldier who has been captured and is kept prisoner by the enemy

reconstruction: a period following a war when the infrastructure of a defeated country is rebuilt, especially with the aid of the victor

weapons of mass destruction (WMDs): weapons—generally chemical, biological, or nuclear weapons—that kill large numbers of people over a long period of time

WHO'S WHO?

Dr. Iyad Allawi (b. 1946)
Dr. Iyad Allawi was born in Baghdad. He was educated as a medical doctor and joined the Baath Party in 1961. Ten years later, he fled into exile in London. In 1978 assassins sent by Saddam tried to murder him. As a result of wounds, Allawi was in the hospital for almost a year. As member of a prominent Shiite family, he was chosen to be interim prime minister of Iraq in June 2004.

Huda Salih Mahdi Ammash (b. 1953)
Huda Salih Mahdi Ammash was born in Iraq. She was one of Saddam Hussein's top advisers. She received master's and doctoral degrees in microbiology in the United States. Later, it was said that she worked on the development of biological weapons, earning her the nickname "Ms. Anthrax." She was captured by coalition forces and taken into custody in May 2003.

L. Paul Bremer III (b. 1941)
L. Paul Bremer was born in Hartford, Connecticut. He received his bachelor's degree from Yale and earned graduate degrees at the University of Paris and at Harvard. In the 1980s, President Reagan named him ambassador at large for counterterrorism, and he became chairman of the National Commission on Terrorism in 1999. He was appointed the chief U.S. official in Iraq in May 2003. In August 2003, Bremer named the 25-member Iraqi Governing Council and later oversaw the writing of a new constitution.

George Herbert Walker Bush (b. 1924)
George H. W. Bush was born in Massachusetts. When he was 18, he joined the navy and became a fighter pilot in World War II. Bush attended Yale University, then worked in the oil industry in Texas. He served two terms as a congressman from Texas. Later, he was named ambassador to the United Nations and chief of the CIA. He served as vice president under Ronald Reagan from 1981 to 1989. He was elected the 41st president of the United States in 1988. As president, he was commander in chief of the U.S. armed forces during Operations Desert Shield and Desert Storm.

George Walker Bush (b. 1946)
George W. Bush was born in New Haven, Connecticut. He grew up in Texas and went to Yale. Later, he married Laura Welch, and they have two daughters. Bush was governor of Texas from 1995 to 2001 and was elected the 43rd president of the United States in 2000. The attacks on the World Trade Center in New York and on the Pentagon in Washington, D.C., on September 11, 2001, occurred during his presidency. Since then, Bush has focused on battling terrorism at home and abroad.

Rhonda Cornum (b. 1955)
Rhonda Cornum was born in Dayton, Ohio, and grew up in East Aurora, New York. She studied medicine and received a PhD in biochemistry from Cornell University.

Cornum joined the army when she was 23. When the Gulf War broke out, Major Cornum went to the Gulf as an officer and a flight surgeon. She was injured and became the first female U.S. prisoner of war. In addition to being a medical doctor and an army officer, Colonel Cornum is also a qualified pilot and paratrooper.

Adnan Pachachi (b. 1923)

Adnan Pachachi was born in Baghdad. Pachachi was a foreign minister in Iraq's pre–Baath Party government and belongs to one of the country's best-known Sunni families. In 1971 Pachachi went into exile in the United Arab Emirates (UAE). He served as president of the Iraqi Governing Council in late 2003 and early 2004. He turned down the ceremonial position of president of Iraq.

Colin Powell (b. 1937)

General Colin Powell was born in and grew up in New York City. He attended City College of New York, where he joined the Reserve Officer's Training Corps. He continued in the military after he graduated. Later Powell earned an MBA from George Washington University. In 1989 he became the first African American to become chairman of the Joint Chiefs of Staff, and he served until 1993. He and the joint chiefs were in charge of U.S. forces during Operations Desert Shield and Desert Storm. He retired from the military in 1993 and was appointed secretary of state in 2001.

Saddam Hussein (b. 1937)

Saddam Hussein ruled Iraq as a dictator from 1979 to 2003. He was born in a village near Tikrit, and his early life was influenced by the violence of his abusive stepfather and a bigoted uncle. Saddam's rule was marked by bloodshed, terror, and genocide (the murder of people based on their ethnicity or religion). He created one of the most powerful militaries in the world and used it to control his own people, to fight Iran, and to invade Kuwait. He was captured by U.S. troops in December 2003.

H. Norman Schwarzkopf (b.1934)
H. Norman Schwarzkopf was born in Trenton, New Jersey. Schwarzkopf attended the U.S. Military Academy at West Point. He joined the army and later earned a master's degree from the University of Southern California. He served twice in the Vietnam War and became commander in chief of the U.S. Central Command, in charge of all of the U.S. forces in the Middle East, in 1988. His role in Desert Storm earned him the nickname "Stormin' Norman." Schwarzkopf retired in 1991 after the end of Operation Desert Storm.

Grand Ayatollah Ali Sistani (b. 1930)

Grand Ayatollah Ali Sistani was born in Meshad, Iran, and moved to Najaf, Iraq, in 1952. Because he has achieved the rank of marja (supreme religious scholar), Shiite Muslims throughout the world look to him for moral guidance. He has urged Iraqis not to resort to violence. He supports giving Islam a special place under new Iraqi laws but opposes an Iranian-style religious government.

SOURCE NOTES

16 "Winds of Death: Iraq's Use of Poison Gas against Its Kurdish Population," Physicians for Human Rights, February 1989, <http://www.phrusa.org/research/iraq/winds _methods.html> (October 13, 2003).

20 Kemal Bosnak, e-mail message to author, August 6, 2003.

20 Otto Friedrich, ed. *Desert Storm: The War in the Persian Gulf* (Boston: Little, Brown and Company, 1991), 26.

27 Jadranka Porter, *Under Siege in Kuwait: A Survivor's Story* (Boston: Houghton Mifflin, 1991), 37.

29 "Text of U.N. Iraq Resolution." *CBSNEWS.com,* November 8, 2002, <http://www.cbsnews.com/ stories/2002/11/08/national/main528675.shtml> (February 23, 2004).

29 "The Gulf War. Oral History: Tariq Aziz," *PBS Online & WGBH/Frontline,* n.d., <http://www .pbs.org/wgbh/pages/frontline/gulf/oral/aziz/3 .html> (May 21, 2003).

29 Rod McQueen, "Swift Strikes a Success: Iraqi Air Force 'Decimated' as Saddam's Elite Guard Hit," *Financial Post* (Toronto), January 17, 1991, sect. 1.

36 "The Gulf War: Oral History: Tariq Aziz," *PBS Online & WGBH/Frontline,* n.d., <http://www .pbs.org/wgbh/pages/frontline/gulf/oral/aziz/2 .html> (May 21, 2003).

38 Youssef Abdul-Moati, ed., *A Diary of an Iraqi Soldier* (Almansoria, Kuwait: Center for Research and Studies on Kuwait, 1994), 15.

38 Friedrich, 50.

39 David Frost, "Interview with General Schwarzkopf on Gulf War Aftermath," *USA Today,* September 3, 1996, <http://www.usatoday .com/news/index/iraq/nirq053.htm> (October 13, 2003).

42 Philip Shenon, "Soldiers Wonder How Bad It Will Be," *New York Times,* January 16, 1991, A12.

44 Phillip Thompson, *Into the Storm: A U.S. Marine in the Persian Gulf War* (Jefferson, NC: McFarland & Company, Inc., 2001), 171.

49 Michael R. Gordon and General Bernard E. Trainor, *The Generals' War: The Inside Story of the Conflict in the Gulf* (Boston: Little, Brown and Company, 1995), 450.

56 "President Delivers State of the Union Address," *The White House,* January 29, 2002, <http://www.whitehouse.gov/news/releases/ 2002/01/20020129-11.html> (August 4, 2004).

60 "Interview with International Wire Services," *U.S. Department of State,* March 18, 2003, <http://www.state.gov/secretary/rm/2003/ 18810.htm> (August 4, 2004).

68 "Bush Makes Historic Speech aboard Warship," *CNN.com,* May 1, 2003, <http://www .cnn.com/2003/US/05/01/bush.transcript/ index.html> (August 4, 2004).

74 Roula Khalaf, "UAE Says Helping Rebuild Iraq Will Hasten Troops' Exit," *Financial Times,* October 2, 2003, 6.

77 Jerry Harben, "Medical Personnel Answer the Call in Iraq," *The Mercury,* June 2003, <http:// www.armymedicine.army.mil/news/mercury/ 03-06/iraq.htm> (October 7, 2003).

77 Jerry Harben, "Iraqi Freedom Shows Value of Early Care," *The Mercury,* July 2003, <http:// www.armymedicine.army.mil/news/mercury/ 03-07/iraq.cfm> (October 10, 2003).

84 Robin Wright, "Iraqis Back New Leaders, Poll Says," *Washington Post,* June 25, 2004, A19. Reprinted on the Web at <http://www .washingtonpost.com/wp-dyn/articles/ A3433-2004Jun24.html> (August 17, 2004).

84 Dan Murphy, "Quiet Handover, Secret Ceremony," *Christian Science Monitor,* June 29, 2004.

84 "Iraqi Press Headlines and Quotes," *BBC Monitoring Newsfile,* June 29, 2004.

84 "Iraqi Premier Blames 'Muslim Countries' for Funding Iraq Resistance," *BBC Monitoring Middle East,* August 2, 2004.

SELECTED BIBLIOGRAPHY, FURTHER READING, & WEBSITES

SELECTED BIBLIOGRAPHY

Abdul-Moati, Youssef, ed. *A Diary of an Iraqi Soldier.* (Almansoria, Kuwait: Center for Research and Studies on Kuwait, 1994).

Allen, Thomas B., F. Clifton Berry, and Norman Polmar. *CNN War in the Gulf.* Atlanta: Turner Publishing Company, 1991.

Alvord, Valerie. "Non-citizens Fight and Die for Adopted Country." *USA Today.* April 8, 2003. <http://www.usatoday.com/news/world/iraq/2003-04-08-noncitizen-usat_x.htm> (August 27, 2004).

Apple, R. W., Jr. "Allies Destroy Iraqis' Main Force; Kuwait Is Retaken after 7 Months." *The New York Times,* February 28, 1991. <http://partners.nytimes.com/1991/02/28/international/worldspecial/28IRAQ.htl> (n.d.).

Blair, Arthur H. *At War in the Gulf: A Chronology.* College Station: Texas A&M University Press, 1992.

Bragg, Rick. *I Am a Soldier, Too: The Jessica Lynch Story.* New York: Alfred A. Knopf, 2003.

Cornum, Rhonda. *She Went to War: The Rhonda Cornum Story.* Novato, CA: Presidio, 1992.

Dunnigan, James F., and Austin Bay. *From Shield to Storm: High-Tech Weapons, Military Strategy, and Coalition Warfare in the Persian Gulf.* New York: William Morrow and Company, 1992.

Friedrich, Otto, ed. *Desert Storm: The War in the Persian Gulf.* Boston: Little, Brown and Company, 1991.

Gordon, Michael R., and General Bernard E. Trainor. *The Generals' War: The Inside Story of the Conflict in the Gulf.* Boston: Little, Brown and Company, 1995.

Harben, Jerry, ed. "Iraqi Freedom Shows Value of Early Care." *The Mercury.* July 2003. <http://www.armymedicine.army.mil/news/mercury/03-07/iraq.cfm> (August 27, 2004).

Houlahan, Thomas. *Gulf War: The Complete Story.* New London, NH: Schrenker Military Publishing, 1991.

Kramer, Samuel Noah. *The Sumerians: Their History, Culture, and Character.* Chicago: University of Chicago Press, 1963.

Lunaville.com. "Iraq Coalition Casualty Count." October 12, 2003. <http://icasualties.org/oif/> (August 27, 2004).

Murray, Williamson, and Major General Robert H. Scales Jr. *The Iraq War: A Military History.* Cambridge, MA: Harvard University Press, 2003.

Porter, Jadranka. *Under Siege in Kuwait: A Survivor's Story.* Boston: Houghton Mifflin, 1991.

Sifry, Micah L., and Christopher Cerf, eds. *The Iraq War Reader: History, Documents, Opinions.* New York: Touchstone, 2003.

Women in Military Service for America Memorial Service Foundation, Inc. *Voices: Native American Women in the US Armed Forces.* n.d. <http://www.womensmemorial.org/historyandcollections/aboutus/natamiva.html> (n.d.)

Worsnip, Patrick. "Saddam's Iron Grip on Power." In *Saddam's Iraq: Face-Off in the Gulf.* Upper Saddle River, NJ: Reuters Prentice Hall, 2003.

FURTHER READING

Anderson, Dale. *Saddam Hussein.* Minneapolis: Lerner Publications Company, 2004.

Finlayson, Reggie. *Colin Powell.* Minneapolis: Lerner Publications Company, 2004.

Márquez, Herón. *George W. Bush.* Minneapolis: Lerner Publications Company, 2002.

Sherman, Josepha. *The Cold War.* Minneapolis: Lerner Publications Company, 2004.

Woolf, Alex. *Osama bin Laden.* Minneapolis: Lerner Publications Company, 2004.

WEBSITES

Air Force Fact Sheets: Air Force Assets
<http://www.af.mil/factsheets/>
This site contains air force fact sheets on many subjects, including planes, weapons, and operations.

Arab American Institute: Americans, Iraqis Discuss War
<http://www.aaiusa.org/davidson_baghdad.htm>
Two programs feature students of Baghdad University and U.S. students at Davidson College discussing the 2003 war with Iraq.

The Gulf War
<http://www.pbs.org/wgbh/pages/frontline/>
The files of the television news program *Frontline* on PBS contain a number of programs about events during the Iraqi wars.

The White House
<http://www.whitehouse.gov/>
This site gives news of White House activities, including the texts of presidential speeches, as well as announcements and text of talks and appearances by other government officials.

INDEX

ABOUT THE AUTHORS

Lawrence J. Zwier is an administrator and lecturer at Michigan State University. He has published several books on current events and other topics. He lives in Okemos, Michigan, with his wife, Jean, and their two children, Maryn and Robbie.

Matthew S. Weltig is a lecturer at the University of Nevada. He has lived and taught in Korea, Japan, Turkey, and the United States. He currently lives in Reno, Nevada, with his wife.

PHOTO ACKNOWLEDGMENTS

The images in this book are used with the permission of: © Patrick Robert/ CORBIS SYGMA, pp. 4–5, 66 top; © Nik Wheeler/CORBIS, p. 6; University of Minnesota Special Collections and Archives, p. 8; © Burstein Collection/CORBIS, p. 9; Library of Congress, p. 10 top (LC-USZ62-121164); © Hulton-Deutsch Collection/CORBIS, p. 10 bottom; © Bettmann/CORBIS, pp. 11, 15; © Keystone Press/ZUMA Press, p. 12; © Francoise de Mulder/CORBIS, pp. 14, 49; © Howard Davies/CORBIS, p. 16; © Yann Arthus-Bertrand/CORBIS, p. 18; George Bush Presidential Library, pp. 23, 24, 39, 90C; Defense Visual Information Center (DVIC), pp. 25, 31 top, 40, 42, 43 top, 45, 64 both, 76, 91 C; U.S. Air Force, Msgt. Kit Thompson, pp. 26, 47; © Patrick Durand/CORBIS SYGMA, p. 28; SPCA Robert Elliot, U.S. Army, p. 31 bottom; U.S. Navy, PHZ Susan Carl, p. 35; © Anthony Suau/Liaison/Getty Images, pp. 37, 41; JOI Joe Gawlowicz, U.S. Navy, p. 38; © Scott Peterson/Getty Images, p. 43 bottom; © Jacques Langevin/CORBIS SYGMA, p. 44; © Shepard Sherbell/CORBIS SABA, p. 48; © Barry Iverson/Time Life Pictures/Getty Images, p. 50; © Art Directors, p. 51; © Iraqi News Agency/ ZUMA Press, p. 52; © CORBIS/SYGMA, p. 53; Andrea Booher/FEMA, p. 54; U.S. Marines, p. 55; © Reuters/CORBIS, pp. 58, 67; © Ahmed al Rubayyh/Getty Images, p. 59; © Bill Pugliano/Getty Images, p. 60; U.S. Naval Photos provided by Navy Visual News Service, Washington, D.C., p. 61; United States Air Force, pp. 63 top, 81; © Scott Nelson/Getty Image, p. 66 bottom; © Stephen JAFFE/AFP/ Getty Images, p. 68; © Todd Strand/Independent Picture Services, pp. 70 top, 80, 91 B; © PPS Vienna/ZUMA Press, p. 70 bottom; © SABAH ARAR/AFP/Getty Images, p. 72; © ROBERT SULLIVAN/AFP/Getty Images, p. 73; © Al Arabiya/ Reuters/CORBIS, p. 74; © Guillermo Navarro/COVER/CORBIS, p. 75; © Kimamasa Mayama/Reuters/CORBIS, p. 78; © Brooks Kraft/CORBIS, p. 79; Staff Sgt. D. Myles Cullen, U.S. Airforce/United States Department of Defense, pp. 82-83; © Cris Bouroncle/Pool/Reuters/CORBIS, p.90A; © Courtesy Department of Defense/ZUMA Press, p. 90 B; Department of Defense, p. 90 D; Department of the Army, p. 91 A. Maps by Laura Westlund, pp. 7, 30, 62;

Front cover: © Joe Raedle/Getty Images.